Landing Your First Job

Andrea Shavick

KOGAN PAGE

For Daniel, Graham and Mark

YOURS TO HAVE AND TO HOLD
BUT NOT TO COPY

First published in 1999

Apart from any fair dealing for the purposes of research or private study, or criticism or review, as permitted under the Copyright, Designs and Patents Act 1988, this publication may only be reproduced, stored or transmitted, in any form or by any means, with the prior permission in writing of the publishers, or in the case of reprographic reproduction in accordance with the terms and licences issued by the CLA. Enquiries concerning reproduction outside these terms should be sent to the publishers at the undermentioned address:

Kogan Page Limited
120 Pentonville Road
London N1 9JN

© Andrea Shavick, 1999

The right of Andrea Shavick to be identified as the author of this work has been asserted by her in accordance with the Copyright, Designs and Patents Act 1988.

British Library Cataloguing in Publication Data

A CIP record for this book is available from the British Library.

ISBN 0 7494 2858 9

Typeset by Kogan Page Ltd
Printed and bound by Clays, St Ives plc

Contents

Acknowledgements ix

Chapter 1 What Sort of Person Are You? 1
How to Find Out What Sort of Work You'd Enjoy? 2; What About Money? 3; Your Salary Expectations: the Reality 4; How to Research Salaries 4; Job Satisfaction 5; Dispelling Those Preconceived Ideas 6; How to Research Careers 6

Chapter 2 What's Out There? 8
Local Papers 8; National Papers 9; Specialist and Trade Magazines 10; Graduate Newspapers 10; Recruitment Fairs 11; The Milk Round 12; The Big Graduate Employers 13; Small to Medium Sized Enterprises 13; SME Recruitment Fairs 14; Careers Offices 15; Recruitment Agencies 15; Networking 16; The Key to Successful Networking 17

Chapter 3 The Internet 18
Who's on the Internet? 18; Where to Start 19; Employer Sites 21; How to Access a Specific Site 22; On-line Application Forms 23; Sending Your CV by E-mail 24; Using E-mail to Apply for Jobs 'on Spec' 25; What if I Don't Have Internet Access? 28; What if I Don't Have an E-mail Address? 28; Do I Have to Apply For a Job On-line? 29

Chapter 4 Make Yourself a Better Prospect 30
What Sort of Work to Go For 30; When to Start 30; Working as Part of Your Course 31; Holiday Work 31; Doing it For 'Free' 31; Charity and Volunteer Work 32

Chapter 5 Researching the Company 33
Why it's Worthwhile 33; How to Research 34; Finding Out What the Employer Wants 35; Researching the Job Itself 36; What if You Don't Like What You Find? 36

Chapter 6 Making Contact and Filling in the Forms 37
Contact by Telephone 37; Application Forms 38; Why Are Application Forms Used? 38; Different Types of Application Forms 38; General Hints on Filling in Application Forms 41; Completing Application Forms on the Spot 42

Contents

Chapter 7   The Telephone Interview — 44
Why Telephone Interviews Exist 44; When Will it Happen? 45; How to Prepare 45; What About the Call Itself? 46; More Dos and Don'ts 47; Body Language 48; Your Objective 48

Chapter 8   The Covering Letter — 50
Presentation: the Art of Looking Good 50; Layout 53; The Content of Your Covering Letter 53; Do Application Forms Need Covering Letters? 56; Words of Warning 56

Chapter 9   Preparing Your CV: Style and Format — 58
The General Appearance of Your CV 58; Should Your CV Be Hand-written? 60; Should Your CV Be Typed? 60; Should Your CV Be Printed? 61; How Long Should a CV Be? 61; Keeping Your Document Together 62

Chapter 10   Preparing Your CV: The Content — 63
Personal Details 63; Education 68; Work Experience 68; Other Skills 69; Interests and Activities 70; Salary Requirements 71; References 72; Being Truthful 73; CV Writing Services 74

Chapter 11   Applying for Jobs 'On Spec' — 76
What Size Organization to Target 76; Do Organizations Take on Staff They're Not Looking For? 77; Where to Start 77; Preparation 78; What About the Actual Approach? 79; Physically Knocking on the Door 80; Telephoning 81; Writing 85; Sending an E-mail 86

Chapter 12   How Applications Are Processed: The Reality — 89
The Dream 89; The Reality 89; What Really Happens 89; The Good News 90; I Haven't Heard Anything – Now What? 91; Tracking Your Application 92

Chapter 13   Modern Recruitment Techniques — 93
Why are These Methods Used? 93; Who Uses Them? 94; Psychometric Tests 94; Verbal Reasoning 94; Numerical Reasoning 97; Personality Questionnaires 100; Other Psychometric Tests 101; In Tray Exercises 104; Group Exercises 106; Group Exercises That Require Technical Know-how 108; Problem-solving Exercises 109; Presentations 110; Using Audio-visual Aids 114; Work Experience 116; Future Developments 117

Chapter 14   Preparing for Your Interview — 118
What Sort of Interview Will it Be? 119; Researching 121; How to Dress 122; What to Take With You 123; Planning the Journey 125; Chickening Out 125; Punctuality – Being Late 125; Punctuality   Arriving Too Early 128

Chapter 15   The Interview Begins — 126
Arriving 127; How to Treat People Other Than Your Interviewer 127;

While You're Waiting 128; Changes in Schedule 128; The Introduction 128; Where to Sit 129; The Handshake 130; Body Language 131; Eye Contact 132; Annoying Mannerisms 132; Your Interviewer's Body Language 133; Swearing 133; How to Address Your Interviewer 133; Smoking 134; Asking For a Drink 134; Accepting a Drink 134; Going Out For a Meal 135; Claiming Expenses: a Warning 135

Chapter 16   Key Questions You Will Be Asked   135
Why are the Answers Important to Me? 136; The Most Popular Questions 137; Commitment Related Questions 140; Competency Related Questions 141; Trick Questions 143; What if I Don't Understand the Question? 144; What if I Can't Think of an Answer? 145; Questions They're Not Allowed to Ask 145; Sexual Discrimination 146; Discrimination Against People With Disability 147; Racial Discrimination 148

Chapter 17   Games Interviewers Play   148
How is Your Interviewer Feeling? 149; Is There Anyone Who Won't be Concerned About My Ambition? 151; What if I Can't Work Out Where My Interviewer Stands? 151; Games Interviewers Play 152

Chapter 18   Even More Successful Interview Techniques   154
Convince Your Interviewer That You Really Want the Job 155; Turn the Interview into a Conversation 157; Ask Questions 158; What Not to Ask 160; What Happens if I Ask Too Many Questions? 161; Make Notes 161; Smile 162; Make Eye Contact 162; Ask For Your Interviewer's Business Card 162; Meeting Other Employees: How to Behave 162; Ask For the Order 163; Things That Turn Employers off Immediately 165; Explaining Previous Bad Work Experiences 165

Chapter 19   Afterwards   166
Be True to Yourself 167; Tracking Your Application 168; Ask for Feedback 168; More Ideas on What to Say 169; Reassuring the Employer: Why it's so Important 169; Ask for Another Interview 170

Chapter 20   Your Second Interview   171
So Why do They Want You to Come Back? 172; Preparing For the Second Interview 173; Your Objective 174; What to Say on the Telephone 175; What to Wear 176; The Second Interview Begins 176; Reassuring the Employer That You Are the Right Person 178; Asking for the Order 179; How to End the Second Interview 180

Chapter 21   Creating a Second Chance   180
Failing at the Paper Stage 181; Failing at the Interview Stage 182; Finding Out What Went Wrong 182; What if You Didn't do Anything Wrong? 183; Keeping Your Foot in the Door 183

Contents

Chapter 22 Landing the Job 185
Replying to a Job Offer 186; What if I'm Still Waiting to Hear From Another Organization? 186; Start Dates 187; Salary 187; The 'Perks' 188; Conclusion 189

Further Reading From Kogan Page 190

Index 193

Acknowledgements

My thanks to the following people for their help and advice: Jonathan Watts-Lay and Beverley Bostock of SHL Group Ltd, Jay Snaith and Graham Shavick of Sainsbury's Supermarkets Ltd, Jeremy Langley of The Graduate Recruitment Company, Kristine Howard, Nancy Shavick and the London University Careers Service.

The Lifeplanner Series

There are many situations in life for which your education, your parents or your experience simply have not prepared you. In this major new series, Kogan Page and *The Daily Telegraph* have joined forces with a team of expert writers to provide practical, down-to-earth information and advice for anyone encountering such a situation for the first time.

The series addresses personal finance and consumer issues in a jargon-free, readable way, taking the fear out of planning your life. So whether you are thinking about buying a house, having a baby or just deciding what to spend your first pay cheque on, the Lifeplanner series will help you do so wisely.

Titles available are:

The Young Professional's Guide to Personal Finance
Your First Home: A Practical Guide to Buying and Renting
Making the Most of Being a Student

Forthcoming titles are:

Balancing Your Career, Family and Life
Your First Investment Portfolio
Your Child's Education

Available from all good booksellers. For further information on the series, please contact:

Kogan Page
120 Pentonville Road
London
N1 9JN
Tel. 0171 278 0433
Fax: 0171 837 6348
e-mail: kpinfo@kogan-page.co.uk

1 What Sort of Person Are You?

A few years ago I decided I needed a career change. The conclusion I came to was that since I liked my own company and could sit still for hours, *writing* was the ideal career for me.

But seriously, what about you? What are you good at? What do you like doing? And have you any idea what sort of career you want? Here are some questions to start you thinking...

If you could imagine a perfect working day, what would you be doing?

- Reading and writing?
- Making something?
- Thinking up ideas?
- Helping other people?
- Organizing things?
- Involved in physical activity?
- Finding things out, researching?

Now think about where you would be doing it?

- Indoors, perhaps in an office?
- Outside, in the open air?

- Moving from place to place?
- Close to home, or in the city?

And finally, who you would be working with?

- Lots of other people?
- A small number of people?
- Nobody – you prefer your own company?

Taking a job for the first time is a very big commitment. It's an enormous culture shock if you're not used to it. Working 35 to 40 hours a week (or more in some cases) for many years with relatively little time off, is difficult for even the most dedicated of us. That is why it's so vitally important to do something you enjoy.

How to Find Out What Sort of Work You'd Enjoy

A number of organizations offering career guidance are mentioned in Chapter 3, and some of the best books on the subject are listed in the Further Reading section at the back of the book. In fact, there are no end of tests you can take designed to analyse your personality, your abilities, your motivations, your strengths and weaknesses.

However, I believe the best way to find out what will make you *happy*, is to take a look at your hobbies and interests. How do you choose to spend your free time?

Are you a people person? Are you very sociable, the life and soul of the party? Do you belong to a lot of clubs? Are you always on the phone? Do you hate being by yourself?

If the answer to these questions is 'yes', then look for a career which involves a lot of contact with people. Working with people your own age, perhaps within an organization offering plenty of recreational facilities, would be ideal. Lots of people to talk to, lots of new friends to make – this is where you'll be happiest.

What Sort of Person Are You?

Are you very individualistic? Do you enjoy being by yourself and doing things in your own way? Could you be described as a bit of a loner? Do you enjoy arts and crafts, reading, writing, gardening, or anything else that requires self-motivation and lots of peace and quiet?

If your answer to these questions is 'yes', then look for a career in which you make your own decisions, rather than always having to follow orders. You'll be much happier being self-reliant than trying to fit into a team. If all this sounds a little too lonely, how about a job based in an office, but going out and travelling around?

Are you a team player? Do you play a lot of team sports? Do you depend on other people a lot? Do you dislike making decisions until you've consulted your friends? Do you enjoy being 'one of the crowd?'

If your answers to these questions is 'yes', then look for a career where the ability to get on with other people is an integral part of the job. You are an ideal 'company' man or woman. Fitting in is easy for you because you enjoy the feeling of belonging. Working as part of a team, perhaps on the same project or towards a shared goal, will suit you.

What About Money?

This is a very important consideration when thinking about a career. Obviously, some jobs pay better than others. How important an issue this is depends upon the sort of lifestyle you want, and your future goals in life. Try and forget the expectations your friends and family have of you – how do *you* honestly feel about it?

- Are you very materialistic?

- Do you spend a lot of money on yourself?

- Have you any burning ambitions to own big, expensive houses, fast cars, etc?

Your Salary Expectations: the Reality

When you land your first job, you will probably start on the bottom rung of the salary ladder.

School-leavers, graduates and other first-time job hunters often have a vastly over-inflated idea of the salary they can expect. But before you can command a huge salary, you will need some work experience under your belt.

So, if financial rewards are very important to you, now is the time to investigate salaries within your chosen field. Don't just think about entry-level salaries; investigating your potential earnings in five, or even 10 years time, is just as important.

How to Research Salaries

Here are some ways to find out what level of income your chosen career will provide you with.

- Ask your friends and family. Do they know anyone already working in that field that you could talk to whom?

- Look at recruitment advertising in the press, particularly the trade papers for your chosen profession. At least some of them will state salaries offered.

- Phone companies in your chosen field and ask them. If you're friendly and polite, most organizations will be happy to talk to you. Ask for personnel or human resources to start with. Explain that you're thinking of a career in XYZ profession and could they give you a general idea of the job itself and the salary levels. If they sound friendly, why not ask if you can come along and discuss it with them?

- Speak to recruitment agencies who specialize in that field. Of course, they may be more interested in getting you on their books, but that's okay. You could end up landing a job that way.

What Sort of Person Are You?

- Ask your local Chamber of Commerce. Many of them publish salary statistics.

- Ask the careers office at school/university, or the one in your local area. They will be able to give you the published entry level salaries in many organizations and professions.

- Ring the quality national newspapers. Some of them have reference libraries and will be happy to help.

- Log on to the Internet. Some sites (for example Reed Employment at www.reed.co.uk) have 'salary calculators' which can tell you how much you'd make doing the same job in hundreds of different locations.

Job Satisfaction

Money is important, but for most people in work, it isn't the most important factor when considering how satisfied they are with their jobs. Job satisfaction depends even more upon:

- liking the people you work with;

- feeling respected and valued by your employer;

- feeling that the work you do is meaningful, that it has value;

- finding the journey to work reasonably stress free;

and probably the most important thing of all:

- enjoying the work itself.

If you don't have any of these things, it doesn't matter how enormous your salary is, you'll still be unhappy. So while you're investigating salary levels in your chosen career, why not find out as much as you can about what exactly is involved in the job on a day-to-day basis.

Dispelling Those Preconceived Ideas

Most people have notions about different jobs; what they involve, whether they're interesting or glamorous or boring, not to mention the personal qualities you need to be able to do them. But unless you investigate, your preconceived ideas will be the only ones you'll ever have. For instance:

- You would imagine a bodyguard to be macho, aggressive, and enjoy a good fight – and you would be wrong. Professional bodyguards do have to be tough, but quick-thinking, tact and the ability to *avoid* trouble is much more important.

- And what about accountancy. Aren't all accountants deadly boring? Surely all they do is analyse financial reports and add up numbers? Actually, one of the most important skills needed to be a successful accountant is the ability to get on with people.

- Aren't all salespeople loud, extremely confident, talkative extroverts? The truth is that many sales jobs are rather lonely, often involving a lot of travelling or working from home. The best performers are often quiet, unassuming, self-reliant types with excellent listening skills!

These are three rather extreme examples, but you get the point.

How to Research Careers

Here are some ways to find out what sort of work your chosen career would involve:

- Ask your friends and family. Do they know anyone already working in that field who you could talk to? This is the best way to get a feel for what a job entails.

What Sort of Person Are You?

- Speak to your careers service at school or university. They often have contacts who would be more than happy to talk to you about the work they do.

- Careers services can also put you in touch with the relevant association or society; there is one for practically every single career you can think of.

- Many sites on the Internet provide detailed profiles of every profession that exists.

- Look at recruitment advertising in the press, particularly the trade papers for your chosen profession. What sort of qualities are they looking for in the successful candidate? Could they be describing you?

- Phone companies in your chosen field and ask them. Explain that you're thinking of a career in XYZ profession and could you come and talk to them about what the work involves. Would it be possible to spend some time with somebody who does that job (commonly called 'work shadowing').

- Read careers books; some suggestions are given at the back of the book.

There's no doubt about it; a little self-analysis and a little research *before* you start your job hunt, are absolutely essential. Your future happiness depends upon it.

2 What's Out There?

There are so many places where jobs are advertised, it's hard to know where to start. This chapter will give you a basic run-down of what's on offer, with the exception of the Internet, which is covered in the next one.

Local Papers

Every town has its own local paper. Some have half a dozen. Most of them are published weekly. If you want to work locally, if the idea of commuting into the city doesn't appeal, then perhaps your local paper might hold the answers.

Generally, local papers come in two varieties: the paid-for paper and the free sheet. Both of them usually carry situations vacant advertising for all sorts of jobs, particularly:

- Jobs with the local authority. Everything from nurses, teachers, administrators, youth workers, project workers, and so on, the list is endless.

- Jobs with local firms. Even if a job advertised doesn't appeal, the local paper is a good source of information on which employers are located near you.

- A list of all the local recruitment agencies and the area of work in which they specialize.

Working locally has its attractions:

- Less time spent getting to work.

What's Out There?

■ Less money spent on train fares and petrol.

■ Work colleagues are more likely to live near you, giving you the chance to make new, local friends.

To find out about the local papers in your area, just go to any newsagent, or the local library.

> **Tip:** If you are away at university, but still want to see what's available in your home town, ask your local paper to mail you a copy every week. For a small charge (usually you have to prepay this) you can order a couple of months at a time. Just ring up and ask for the circulation department.

Alternatively, you can view thousands of locally advertised jobs around the UK on the following Internet site: http://www.job-hunter.co.uk/

There is more information on the Internet in the next chapter.

> **Tip:** If you want to find out what local paper exists in any given area, ring the nearest library and ask.

National Papers

These are many and varied; you can inspect them all at any good newsagent or library. As well as having large recruitment sections, they also carry interesting articles on all aspects of the job market.

Some of the 'nationals' specialize in different types of recruitment advertising on different days of the week. Keep looking to

Landing Your First Job

find out when your chosen career is featured. Others produce an extra large supplement once a week. Alternatively, go surfing on the Internet; all the big papers have interesting and informative sites.

Specialist and Trade Magazines

Almost every single type of job title you care to name will not only have its own association or trade body, but its own trade papers and magazines as well. To find out what's published in your chosen field:

- read career books: they often detail trade associations and their publications;

- ask at a large newsagent;

- visit your nearest large reference library and look up *BRAD* which lists every single newspaper and magazine currently available;

- ask your careers service.

> **Tip:** Generally speaking, trade papers will send you out a sample copy free of charge. Ring up and request a 'voucher copy'.

Graduate Newspapers

If you are at university in the UK, you'll already be familiar with *Prospects Today*, the national graduate newspaper which carries plenty of situations vacant advertising. Available on every campus, it's published fortnightly during term time, and weekly during the summer break. Most universities also publish their own career vacancy bulletin on a regular basis.

Recruitment Fairs

Recruitment fairs, job fairs and training exhibitions are usually advertised in the press and on the Internet. School and university careers services are also in the know about forthcoming 'events'. Recruitment fairs can be general in nature, or targeted at specific sections of the job market, ie graduate recruiting, engineering, etc.

Going along to a recruitment fair can be a bit of an eye opener for the job-hunter. All those employers trying to get you interested in *them*. It's nice to be in a buyer's market for a change!

As well as plenty of employers and recruitment agencies to visit, there are usually a number of interesting talks, advice workshops and seminars, offering everything from CV writing skills to career analysis.

Tips for getting the most out of a recruitment fair

- Take plenty of copies of your CV. Keep them in a document folder to ensure they stay clean.

- Pick up a copy of the catalogue. This will detail every employer at the fair, the jobs on offer, and often their individual recruitment procedures.

- Complete application forms carefully. Don't rush, take your time. Alternatively, take the forms home with you; they don't *have* to be handed in on the spot.

- Go in 'interview mode', ie on your best behaviour. Treat the staff on the stands with respect and courtesy – they'll appreciate it. Working at an exhibition is very hard work.

- Write down names so that you can follow up your applications by writing or telephoning the person you spoke to, in a couple of weeks' time. Make sure you get the spelling of their names right.

- Dress smartly. For the main recruitment fairs, business dress is advisable. Besides, you might find yourself being formally interviewed.

- Ask lots of questions. 'Can you tell me about the job?' 'Can you describe a typical day?' 'Do you have a formal job description I can have?' 'What's it like, working for XYZ?' 'Is there anyone I could speak to who does this job?' 'Where are the vacancies?' 'How many positions are you trying to fill?' 'What sort of recruitment process do candidates go through?' 'What sort of qualities are you looking for?'

- Take a notebook to write it all down, and your diary to arrange interviews.

- Enjoy yourself, but work hard too. Look upon the day as a job-hunting exercise, not a chance to drink in the bar. Aim to leave with a lot more information than you went with.

The Milk Round

This is the name for the annual round of recruitment fairs that take place at universities throughout the country where employers go to sign up graduates. All the hints and tips mentioned under recruitment fairs apply.

Every university careers office will be able to tell you what's happening on their campus, just go along and ask. Don't leave it too late; many fairs take place in the first academic term of the year.

Keep an eye on the closing dates for applications too. These should be submitted through your university careers service.

The Big Graduate Employers

Many large organizations have a policy of taking on sizeable numbers of graduates every year, usually for trainee management positions. They tend to follow a set timetable when it comes to their annual recruitment process. Generally, in the UK, these large employers start the ball rolling around September so that's when you need to apply.

The advantages of working for a large organization are considerable. They can offer:

- high starting salaries;

- attractive benefit packages including pensions;

- excellent training programmes;

- excellent career progression;

- an impressive name (and possibly job title) to put on your CV.

But to get all of that you'll have to compete, and the competition is considerable. For example, in the UK the supermarket chain Sainsbury's receives over 40,000 enquiries every year (although only up to 12,000 return their application form) for just 850 trainee manager jobs.

Once the applicants who best meet Sainsbury's criteria have been selected, they are tested and interviewed early in the new year. Successful candidates start their new jobs in September.

But that timetable doesn't apply to every organization – you'll have to ring up and ask the personnel/human resources department of the one you want to work for, and ask.

Small to Medium Sized Enterprises

Before you decide that the only organizations worth working for are big ones, consider the alternative. A smaller company (small to medium enterprise – SME) may have just as much, or even more to offer. (The definition of an SME varies according to who you ask. To give you a rough guide, an SME is usually an organization that employs up to 50 people, and/or a turnover up to £20 million. So 'small' can mean anything from very small, to quite large, well-established and very successful companies.)

Here are just some of the advantages of working for an SME:

- more responsibility, earlier on;

- the chance to work directly with the directors/owners of business;

- greater variety of work;

- the opportunity to learn all aspects of how a business works;

- reasonable starting salaries (SMEs know they have to compete with the big players);

- a real chance to be a big fish in a small pond.

It's also much easier to land a job with an SME than a large company because their recruitment processes are usually simpler. After you've submitted your CV and letter, most SMEs still rely on a couple of interviews to pick their people. And that's it; there's no carefully designed application form with thousands of questions to wade through; no psychometric testing; and no overnight stays in hotels, building Lego bridges and being expected to give professional presentations!

SME Recruitment Fairs

These are recruitment fairs where there are no multinational companies present. All the exhibitors are SMEs. These fairs are growing in popularity because it gives smaller companies the chance to attract staff. Don't ignore an SME fair just because you haven't heard of any of the exhibitors. Go along, and perhaps, leave with an excellent job offer!

Careers Offices

Open to the general public, careers services exist in practically every town or city, with schools and universities running their own services on-site. Some university careers services run their own employment agencies too. A visit is a definite must. Services on offer range from general career advice, to the more specific:

- general reference library facilities;

- employer libraries providing specific employer profiles, company reports, etc;

- help with CVs, letters, application forms and interview techniques;

- weekly job bulletins;

- details of forthcoming recruitment fairs.

Recruitment Agencies

Too many to list, there are literally thousands of agencies out there. Although some of them prefer to take on people with several years' work experience, there are still many who would be delighted to have you on their books. All reputable agencies charge the employer and not the applicant, so you have absolutely nothing to lose by signing up.

Recruitment agencies often specialize in one particular area of employment, such as accountancy, the IT industry, overseas jobs and graduate recruitment, to name but a few. They often offer career advice too. Some agencies only deal with temporary appointments and can be a good place to start when you're looking for part-time or temporary work, for example, in your gap year.

Ask your careers service for some recommendations, look up the *Graduate's Guide to Recruitment Consultants* in your reference or careers library, or just open the papers to see who's out there. Alternatively, on the Internet, try http://www.net.jobs.co.uk for links to hundreds of recruitment agencies. (Agencies can be quite picky about who they take on. Be prepared to go through an initial screening process such as providing your CV and attending an interview – which should be treated as seriously as a job interview.)

Networking

This isn't a place to look, it's more a way of life. Start practising a bit of networking now, and acquire a habit of a lifetime.

Networking simply means asking people you know for help and advice. In terms of getting a job, networking is an indispensable tool with which you simply cannot afford to be without. Use (and improve) your networking skills to find out about job vacancies:

- that already exist;
- that may just be about to open up;
- that will be available in the future; and also
- information about what jobs in your chosen field are really like;
- information about salary levels (covered in Chapter 1).

At the very beginning of your working life there are a lot of people you can ask for help and advice.

Parents – often a valuable source of information. Most parents will do anything they can to help their children. They want you to be successful. They'll willingly pull out all the stops and ring up friends, acquaintances and business contacts; anyone they can think of who might be able to help.

Personal contacts – friends and relatives are also a really good source of information. Don't be afraid to ask. The worst they can say is, 'Sorry, I can't help you.'

Other contacts – the teaching staff at school, college and university, people you've worked for before (even if it was only part-time), professional people in your community, eg your doctor. All these people are valuable sources of information for the determined job-hunter.

The Key to Successful Networking

The greater your experience (and usually the older you get) the more contacts you will make. When you meet new people, make an effort to find out what they do, what they're interested in, who *they* know. Get their business card, write down their telephone number, and keep all the information.

Building up a network of friends, acquaintances and business contacts is a continuous thing, it never stops. Throughout your life, it's always extremely useful to know someone who knows something or someone. Often, it is through networking that many senior never-advertised positions are filled.

The key to successful networking, is to *give* as well as take from your contacts. If somebody you know has a problem, always try and help. Alternatively, search through your list of contacts to find someone who can. Always be on the look out for ways to help the people you know, and to send business their way, without expecting anything in return.

3 The Internet

The Internet is already established as a major medium for job-hunters, which cannot be ignored. At the time of writing there were over 1,376,615 sites on the Internet with 'job' in the title and by the time this book is published, the number will have grown even more.

Who's on the Internet?

As well as a cost-effective way to tell the world about products and services, companies also realize that the Internet is a great place to solve recruitment problems too. So the answer is just about everybody, from your local small business employing two dozen people, to the largest multinational conglomerates employing thousands all round the globe. Even I've got my own site – the address is given later in this chapter.

Many other organizations concerned with recruitment also advertise their wares on the Net:

- recruitment agencies and other employment specialists;

- magazines and newspapers (with their situations vacant columns);

- organizations offering career advice;

- organizations offering psychometric and aptitude testing;

- the trade associations of many different professions.

The Internet

All these and more can all be found on the Internet. Even individual towns and cities are opening up their own Web sites with job advertisements from local organizations. All you need is time to find it all.

Where to Start

Assuming you are reasonably familiar with the Internet, just log on and take a look. Here's a short list of sites that will give you a flavour of what's on offer. They're so easy to use, you'll soon have the confidence to explore further.

http://www.jobhunter.co.uk

Updated daily, this site lists thousands of jobs that are being currently advertised in the local press. All you do is select the local paper for the area in which you want to work (or alternatively the industry sector you're interested in) and scroll down the list of jobs until you find one that interests you.

Many of the jobs advertised request you make contact via the telephone or the mail so you can simply use the site as a good source of information rather than applying on-line.

http://www.monster.co.uk

This large careers site carries a huge range of jobs and is very easy to use. You simply fill in the blank on-line CV with as much information about yourself and your requirements as you want to give, and the site comes up with a long list of suitable vacancies.

Plenty of advice is given on how to write the on-line CV. They also have a password facility, which enables you to retrieve and change your CV whenever you want.

http://www.reed.co.uk

A good site, not only for job listings but careers advice too. You can find out about the employers advertising their vacancies as well as link up to careers and job-hunting sites from all over the globe.

The site also has a 'regional salary calculator' which tells you how much you can earn doing the same job at different locations around the UK.

Many other employment agencies are on the Net. Remember all reputable employment agencies charge the employer. You should never be asked to pay anything.

http://www.careers.lon.ac.uk

The careers service of London University is one of the best university sites at present. You can access advice on CVs and interviews, careers information, holiday work, forthcoming recruitment fairs and so on, the list is endless.

http://www.gradunet.co.uk

A site for graduates looking for work, it lists employers currently recruiting and provides links to their sites.

http://www.graduate-recruitment.co.uk

Another site for job-hunting graduates which is well worth a visit, and they have an impressive client list.

http://www.prospects.csu.man.ac.uk

The excellent Careers Service site lists graduate recruiters and provides details of forthcoming recruitment fairs. It also helps you decide what to do with your degree, and provides very interesting profiles on hundreds of different occupations.

http://www.gti.co.uk

This user-friendly site has plenty of advice on graduate careers and different occupations. Have a laugh reading the 'World's Worst Interview' and the 'World's Worst Covering Letter'.

http://www.shlgroup.com

A market leader in psychometric testing, they also offer career/aptitude testing.

http://internet-solutions.com/itjobs.htm

This site provides links to recruitment agencies specializing in the IT industries.

http://www.ukdirectory.co.uk

This UK directory site covers just about everything from entertainment to travel. The employment section contains links to employers, recruitment agencies and companies offering career guidance, and is user-friendly.

http://www.topjobs.co.uk

A large site with plenty of jobs plus career advice, links to recruitment agencies and professional associations.

Employer Sites

As already mentioned, practically every business seems to be setting up their own Web site. Of course, not every organization uses the Net to recruit staff. Most of them still concentrate on telling the world about themselves and their products. But the number of employers using this medium to recruit is rising rapidly.

Some organizations simply list vacancies, but a growing number offer potential new recruits an enormous amount of information and guidance. It isn't unusual to be given:

- Details of the sort of people they look for, eg abilities, motivations and desirable personality traits. This person specification is often called an employee profile.

Landing Your First Job

- Self-assessment questionnaires and tests designed to help you analyse how well you fit their employee profile. Spending time on this will give you a good indication of your chances of being hired.

- Help and advice with filling in the on-line application forms.

- A complete run-down of the assessment process they operate; very useful to know in advance that you'll be expected to perform a telephone interview and two whole days of tests, exercises and presentations before you even meet an interviewer face-to-face!

- An invitation to register your CV so you can be matched up with current and future vacancies.

Some organizations even give you the opportunity to question existing staff about the trials and tribulations of working for them. Others operate 'chat rooms' and 'discussion groups' so you can discuss topics and world issues relevant to the organization. Don't pass up the opportunity – use it. At the interview stage they could ask you for your opinion on a controversial issue that concerns them, and they'll expect you to have one.

As well as all this, most sites carry a huge amount of information about the organization itself; very useful when composing covering letters or preparing for an interview.

How to Access a Specific Site

Most organizations print their Web site addresses on their catalogues and letterheads. If not, you can always ring them up and ask. Once you're on-line, try a search using the company's name. Or guess: try using www.organization'sname.com or www.organization'sname.co.uk (commonly used by companies in the UK). Remember there is no full stop after com or uk.

On-line Application Forms

Many employers and recruitment agencies expect you to complete their on-line application forms. All you do is type your answers in the boxes. Sounds simple enough. But wait! Before you begin, it's important to take a little time to think about what to say.

Take Your Time

Probably the best thing to do is to print out the application form and have a good look at it off-line. That way you'll be able to prepare well-considered answers without running up a huge telephone bill.

Use Key Words

One of the disadvantages (or advantages) of applying for a job on-line is that it will probably be a computer that looks at your application before an actual person gets their hands on it.

Many employers now use computer software to select the most promising application forms that come in over the Net. What these computer programmes do is scan for key words. Key words are words and phrases that describe your expertise and proficiency, the level of competency you've reached and the skills that you possess.

Look at the advertisement itself for clues about what the employer is seeking. For example, if they want someone who is 'computer literate', it's not enough to say that you are totally capable with computers; that's too vague. Instead, list by name the software packages and the programming languages you've used.

Be specific, and use positive words wherever you can to describe the skills you have. Give the electronic eye of the computer scanning your form something to look at.

Answer all the Questions

You must fill in *all* the boxes – don't leave any blank. If you do, your application may not be processed. If there is a question that you don't want to or need to answer, type n/a in the box.

Sending Your CV by E-mail

Employers and recruitment agencies often leave a blank space on their Web site for you to post your CV into. Although the presentation and content of your paper CV is discussed in Chapters 9 and 10, the CV you send via the Internet necessitates a slightly different approach. Figure 3.1 is an example of a very effective virtual CV.

Tips For Preparing and Submitting CVs By E-mail

Just follow the tips given below:

- To begin with, the person receiving your CV will only be able to see the first few lines. Encourage them to scroll down and read the entire document by catching their attention quickly. Information about skills and capabilities will be more interesting to them than your address, so consider rearranging things so that the most pertinent information appears first.

- An attractive photo of yourself is a good attention-getter.

- To check what your CV looks like on the Net, simply send it to yourself.

- If possible, send your CV as an attached file (employers usually tell you their preferred format in their advertisements). Just in case you ever come up against someone who cannot work out how to 'un-attach' it, keep a plain text file on standby.

On the Net, the text of this CV is white with a purple background, with hypertext appearing in pale yellow. When printed out, the header text is purple (and the main text is grey) on a white background. It looks very smart. You can view this CV on my website: http://www.shavick.com.

Of course, you can do a lot with a little programming knowledge (or the money to pay someone if you can't do it yourself) but producing an attractive and presentable CV for submission via e-mail isn't as hard as it looks.

Using E-mail to Apply For Jobs 'On Spec'

An excellent idea which is discussed in Chapter 11.

Kristine Howard

khoward1@darwin.cc.nd.edu
Pasquerilla West
University of Notre Dame

Resume

KRISTINE HOWARD

22293, Co. Rd. 20
Goshen, IN 46528
khowardl@darwin.cc.nd.edu
http://www.nd.edu/~khoward1

Education

Undergraduate:

- Currently a Senior at the <u>University of Notre Dame</u>, South Bend, Indiana
- Majoring in <u>Film, Television, & Theatre</u>
- B.A. pending graduation May 1999
- Notre Dame Scholar
- Honors Program Student

Secondary:

- Graduated in 1995 from Lakeland High School, Lagrange, Indiana
- Valedictorian (#1 Out of approx. 140 students)
- Indiana Academic Honors Diploma
- National Merit Scholarship winner

Interests and Activities

- Undergraduate:
    - Spent Spring 1998 semester in London, England as part of Notre Dame London Program
    - Created <u>The Roald Dahl Home Page</u> in honor of famous children's author
        - Mentioned in USA Today
    - Volunteered to Create Teamwork for Tomorrow website for community outreach program
    - Member of <u>Pasquerilla West Hall's Women's Interhall Football</u> team
    - Notre Dame Theatre productions
        - "Later Life"-Actor

- "Who's Afraid of Virginia Woolf?" - Stage Manager
- "Lie, Cheat, and Genuflect" - Actor
- "The Grapes of Wrath" - Assistant Stage Manager
- "Dr. Faustus" - Stage Manager
- "Getting Wrecked" - Stage Manager (ND Mainstage Production - World Premiere)
    - Soap Opera Correspondent for campus newspaper, The Observer
- Secondary:
    - Spent Summer 1994 in Krefeld, Germany as part of Indiana University Honors Program in Foreign Languages
    - 3-year member of Speech team
    - 4-year member of Tennis team
    - Amateur Theatre productions
    - President of Student Council
    - Member of National Honor Society
    - Coeditor of school newspaper, The Echo

Work Experience

5/96 – present Coachmen Industries, Inc., Middlebury, Indiana

- Web Designer from 5/97 – 1/98 and 5/98 to present
    - Responsible for creating and maintaining all company websites
        - Examples:
        - Corporation site
        - Coachmen Recreational Vehicle Co.
        - All American Homes
    - Gave Internet presentations at annual Dealer Convention
- Purchasing assistant from 5/96 – 8/96 and 12/96 – 1/97
    - Duties involved data entry, correspondence, file maintenance, and answering telephone

1/96 – 5/97 Office of Information Technologies, University of Notre Dame, South Bend, Indiana

- Quality Improvement Council Secretary
    - Duties involved attending QIC meetings, taking minutes, and posting on website
    - Also assisted Provost's Secretary with various office and Internet tasks

References

Can te provided upon request. E-mail me if interested.

Back to the Main Page

Created and maintained by Kristine Howard, © 1998

Figure 3.1 The virtual CV

What if I Don't Have Internet Access?

Access to the Internet is reasonably easy even if you don't have your own personal computer and Internet account. These are just some of the places where you can go to log on:

Libraries: most large libraries offer Internet access. The disadvantage is that you may find yourself in a queue to use the computer, and it's not very private.

Cybercafes: places where you can eat, drink and socialize as well as surf the Net. Mostly situated in city centres, get a list from *Yellow Pages* or *Internet* magazines.

Schools: a growing number of secondary schools are on the Net. Many offer access to the public; ring your local schools and ask about the facilities they offer.

Universities: all universities are on the Net, and students are provided with their own e-mail address. Access to the public is usually available for a small charge. Ring your nearest one and ask about the facilities they offer.

The major problem for anyone without Internet access is finding somewhere you can spend the time surfing without interruption. To use the Internet you'll need plenty of time, and that won't be easy with a queue of people behind you.

The other thing you'll need is a printer, because you'll definitely find lots of things you'll want to download and print out, such as application forms. So if you're planning to use the local library's computer and printer extensively, perhaps it would be a good idea to offer to provide your own paper. Libraries and schools do not have unlimited resources, so they might be reluctant to let you use too much of them.

What if I Don't Have an E-mail Address?

As mentioned above, colleges and universities are now on the

Net, and it's normal to offer students their own e-mail address, which can be accessed from anywhere in the world.

There are also a growing number of organizations offering free e-mail addresses to anyone who wants one, although you may have to put up with some advertising bumf being sent your way. Just go on-line and do a search under 'free e-mail' and you'll be spoilt for choice.

Do I Have to Apply for a Job On-line?

The majority of employers now expect new staff to come with computer literacy as standard. Certainly, if they are recruiting on the Net, they expect applicants to be conversant with the technology – and not just for jobs in the IT industry either. So if a job advert says, 'Do not snail mail us', you'll know that only applications via e-mail will be accepted.

However, if they also give you their postal address, telephone and fax number, you'll know that it's okay to apply in the traditional way (often disparagingly referred to as the paper option).

Word of Warning

Although the Internet has literally thousands of sites that are of interest, it is not a good idea to use it exclusively in your search for a job.

One thing you do need with the Internet is time. Every site seems to have dozens of link-ups to other sites and before you know it you'll be surfing aimlessly for hours without actually achieving anything. Information can be slow to download during periods of heavy usage (in the UK in the afternoon/evening as users in the USA start logging on) which is why the WWW is often referred to the 'world wide wait'!

Think of the Internet as an excellent source of information, a fast and convenient way to research your chosen organization or career, and then combine it with as many other methods of job-hunting as you possibly can for optimum results!

4 Make Yourself a Better Prospect

A great way to impress potential employers and increase your chances of landing an excellent first full-time job, is to get some part-time, holiday, or placement work experience. Not only will it look good on your CV, it will also prove to an employer that you're serious about your career and the world of full-time work.

What Sort of Work to Go For

Wherever possible, look for work that is relevant to your chosen vocation, ie in the same industry. For example, if you're studying to become a veterinary surgeon, it would make sense to get some experience in a veterinary surgeon's practice, or an animal rescue centre.

Apart from making valuable contacts, one of whom might end up offering you a full-time job, you'll also get a much clearer picture of whether you enjoy the work. If you do, you'll be genuinely enthusiastic and motivated when it comes to the job search. If you hate it, you'll still have time to rethink your career before it's too late.

When to Start

Start as early as possible. If you're planning a gap year, plan to be working through at least part of it. If you're still at university, aim to work though the holidays, including the first one. It's never too early to gain work experience!

Working as Part of Your Course

Many university and college courses offer you the opportunity to take time out to gain work experience, often in the penultimate year of study. Many universities and individual tutors have links with local employers, others offer on-site employment agencies, but generally, it's your responsibility to find a work 'placement', so think carefully about what you want to do and start planning as early as possible.

Holiday Work

Many large companies offer paid work placements during the summer holidays. Applications have to be submitted almost a year in advance, and the competition for places is intense. Ask your careers service for advice as early as you possibly can.

Some employers also offer short 'taster' placements during the Christmas and Easter breaks. Contact the personnel/human resources department of the company you're interested in working for, as early as you possibly can. Even two or three weeks' work experience can be very valuable, both in terms of actual work experience, and the opportunity to make good contacts.

Listings of organizations who offer holiday work both in the UK and abroad can also be found in your local library, and reference library. There are too many books to list. Just go along and have a look. Again, the more relevant your work experience to your chosen vocation, the better.

Doing it For 'Free'

If you can afford to offer your services for free (although expenses and travel costs should be reimbursed) then plenty of companies will be delighted to snap you up!

Although you won't be paid, a large organization should put on a programme for you worth its weight in gold (well, in experience anyway). For instance, if you're aiming to become a buyer for a food retailer, you could end up being taken on supplier visits, visiting food fairs, and working on all sorts of interesting projects.

You'll gain lots of relevant experience and meet all sorts of people in the organization. If they like you, you're much more likely to be taken on when you apply for a permanent position.

Charity and Volunteer Work

Generally, employers are impressed by people who have experience of charity and volunteer work because they feel it demonstrates maturity, as well as simply being a worthy thing to do.

Charities, voluntary organizations and local authorities always have plenty of opportunities available, wherever you live. Ring them up and ask what's available and how you can help.

If you want to combine voluntary work with overseas travel, the careers service, your local library and the Internet, are all good places to find out what's available. On the Internet, try the BUNAC's site at http://www.bunac.org.uk/ to start you off on your search.

Again, wherever possible, make your experience relevant to your chosen vocation. For instance, if you plan to teach, a scheme that gave you the opportunity to help or teach children in a deprived area of the world would be ideal. But be prepared to pay for travel and living accommodation; overseas charity work doesn't come cheap.

5 Researching the Company

Another way to make yourself a better prospect is to do some research.

Why it's Worthwhile

Successful investors wouldn't dream of buying shares before they'd thoroughly investigated the product, or experienced the service a company offered. Why should you be any different? You are about to invest *yourself*, so doing some research isn't just a sensible precaution, it's an absolute necessity!

As far as landing a job is concerned, finding out all you can about the organization you are applying to is probably the single most important thing you can do to increase your chances of success. The reasons are simple.

- The information you acquire can be used to enhance your application: everything from the application form, your CV, and your covering letter, to the answers you give at interview (and the questions you *ask* too).

- Employers are extremely flattered by applicants who take the trouble to find out about their companies. Everyone likes to feel good about themselves and employers are no different. It also impresses *them*. It demonstrates resourcefulness and determination.

■ Employers are looking for people who want to work for them. Demonstrating an interest in their organization will show you are serious about your choice of employer.

And last:

■ Very, few people bother to do it. If you do, you'll stand out from the crowd.

How to Research

Researching is easier than you think. Your goal is to discover as much as you can about the organization you're interested in working for, and there are lots of ways to do it. Here are just a few suggestions.

■ If the organization has a presence on the high street, go along to your nearest branch and have a look round. What do you think of them? Are you impressed? Do they offer a service that you can try out?

If you like what you see, make a note of what it was that impressed you. Was it the products, the merchandise, the professionalism of the staff, the service offered? Whatever it was, write it down.

■ If the organization sells a product to the public (anything from ice cream to newspapers to baby buggies) go along to wherever it's sold and have a look. If it's ice cream, try some! If it's a newspaper, buy a copy!

What do you think of it? Are you impressed? And are there any leaflets you can pick up that give you more information?

■ Ask the organization itself. Telephone and ask for information. Can they send you a brochure, a catalogue, a staff magazine?

If they ask why you want the information, tell them the

truth. 'I'm interested in working for you, and I'd like to find out as much as I can before I apply.'

- If they have one, look at their web site. Take your time. Explore the whole site. Does the department to which you're applying also have its own page?
   Chapter 3 tells you a lot more about what you can discover using the Internet, and it doesn't necessarily mean having to apply on-line. For the purposes of researching, just go surfing and see what you find.

- Look at the organization's advertising. Where do they advertise? What do they advertise? Do they maintain a high profile? What sort of image are they trying to promote?
   Do you like what you see?

Finding Out What the Employer Wants

Look at the organization's situations vacant advertising as well as their general advertising. Read about the qualities and motivations they are looking for in new recruits. Does any of it describe you?

- Get a job description (or job spec) and, if it's available, an applicant profile. This can also be called a 'person specification'. Ring up and ask.

- If you're using a recruitment agency, ask them for a job spec and an applicant profile.

An applicant profile is a list of qualities that the organization thinks the successful applicant will possess. If you know what they're looking for, for example 'flexibility', 'must work well with other team members', you'll know whether it sounds like the right job for you, and which of your strengths to emphasize when you apply.

Researching the Job Itself

Telephone and ask about the job. 'I'm applying for the post of... and I thought I would call you up to find out a little more about it and what's involved before I send you my CV.'

If you can, speak to the person who will be your boss if you get the job. Doing this creates an immediate rapport with them. They'll perceive you as serious and interested, and be very impressed. Hardly anyone else will have bothered to ring them up.

Immediately, you as an applicant, gain a huge advantage over everyone else. Yours is the application that is keenly awaited. You are the person they'll be looking forward to meeting.

Only by researching, will you be able to answer questions like 'Why do you want the job?' and 'Why are you suited to this job?' with genuine sincerity. Only by researching, will you be able to ask informed, relevant and intelligent questions, and every employer knows this. The truth is out there – all you need to do is go and find it!

What if You Don't Like What You Find?

After you've done a little researching, the unexpected may happen. You might decide that you don't want to work for this organization after all. And that's the greatest and most valuable benefit of researching. Apart from helping you land a job, it can also prevent you from making a terrible mistake.

6 Making Contact and Filling in the Forms

Advertisements in newspapers and magazines usually expect you to make contact by letter or telephone. Follow the instructions. If you're asked for a CV and a covering letter, that's what you send. This may sound obvious, but for some strange reason, there are people who only send their name and address and a little note stating, 'I'm brilliant – contact me and find out!' and nothing else.

Naturally, for most employers, this is a complete turn-off. The only thing this 'clever' tactic will achieve is an immediate rejection.

Contact by Telephone

If the advertisement has a name, address *and* telephone number, ring them up. Although you'll probably still have to send a CV or complete an application form, making first contact by telephone has two advantages. The first is that you get a chance to introduce yourself (and hopefully make a good impression). The second is that you get a chance to ask questions.

The information you discover can then be used to tailor your covering letter, or even alter your CV slightly. Your letter will also be more personal, since you'll be able to refer to the things you discussed during the call. You'll even be able to say how pleased you were to speak to them, because now you're even more enthusiastic about the job.

If an advertisement requests you telephone, and all you get is an answerphone, don't put the phone down. Leave a message.

The person in charge of recruiting will definitely get back to you. The answerphone is just a cheap and convenient way to collect all the names, addresses and telephone numbers.

Application Forms

The vast majority of companies now use application forms as part of their recruitment process. For many, the application form is the very first stage. Whether you telephoned, sent a letter, or logged on to their Web site, you can't progress any further until you've filled in the form.

Why are Application Forms Used?

The quick answer is that the advantages (to the employer) are difficult to ignore. Here are some of them, as seen from their point of view.

- Processing application forms is quicker than reading CVs because the questions are laid out in a standardized format.

- Direct comparison of applicants is possible because everyone has to answer the same questions.

- *They* choose the questions. With a CV, it's the *candidate* who decides what to put in, and what to leave out.

- A completed application form will provide a formal record, which may come in handy once the candidate is hired.

Different Types of Application Forms

Application forms vary from company to company. Some only ask a few questions, others want to know everything about you. There are three different types of questions you could be faced

Making Contact and Filling in the Forms

with (and quite often you'll get all three on the same application form).

- First are the basic questions: your name, address, contact numbers, position you are applying for, area you want to work, educational qualifications and work experience.

- Next comes the blank boxes where you are expected to answer questions like, 'Please explain why you are interested in position of XYZ'. If you are applying for a management or trainee management role, you will probably be asked a number of competency based questions as well.

Here are some examples of competency based questions:

Describe a situation where you demonstrated your ability to provide a service to others. What did you do?

Here, the organization is trying to find out whether you will consider and give priority to the needs of its customers.

Describe how you have worked in a team or group situation. How did you contribute to the success of the team?

Here, the organization is clearly looking for someone who can work with other people, share information and recognize the benefits of working towards a common goal.

Obviously, you need to think long and hard about your answers, but you can see that the point of asking these questions is to ascertain how you will behave if you get the job. 'Competency' questions are covered in greater detail in Chapter 16.

- The third type of question you could come up against is the multiple choice. These are easy to spot because you usually get a list of statements with which you have to agree or disagree. Sometimes you'll be asked to rate your agreement or disagreement on a scale of say, one to five.

Landing Your First Job

Your answers will be marked by a computer (although by law, the *decision* about who is successful has to be made by a person).

MOTIVATIONAL QUESTIONNAIRE – To be completed by all applicants

This questionnaire is designed to identify your approach to work-related issues and your preferences for a working environment.

- Please examine each statement carefully. If you agree with it or feel that it is true for you, fill in the circle in the 'AGREE' column. If you disagree with it or it is untrue for you, fill in the 'DISAGREE' column.
- Only if you find the answer is completely impossible for you, fill in the circle in the 'UNSURE' column.
- Please answer these questions to reflect how you actually are, rather than how you would like to be seen.
- Please make sure you answer ALL 28 questions, by fully completing the circle, ie ●

	AGREE	UNSURE	DISAGREE
1. I like to work with the same group every day	O	O	O
2. Every crisis brings the satisfaction of solving it	O	O	O
3. I like to be free to make my own decisions	O	O	O
4. I like to work out why people buy things	O	O	O
5. I don't really get excited about food	O	O	O
6. I like to work with complex data	O	O	O
7. I like lots of time to think about problems	O	O	O
8. I am usually satisfied with the way a shop is being run	O	O	O
9. I like to direct the work of others	O	O	O
10. I don't know enough about food to know what people will like	O	O	O
11. When I see things in shops I get ideas for sales	O	O	O
12. I find numerical problem solving stimulating	O	O	O
13. I occasionally have to upset people to get what I want	O	O	O
14. I am slow but deliberate in my decisions	O	O	O
15. I would love to work in a comfortable office	O	O	O
16. I find computer systems fascinating	O	O	O
17. I would rather give orders than take them	O	O	O
18. I am more likely to buy from a display which is different in some way	O	O	O
19. I enjoy hearing about new recipes for meals	O	O	O
20. I like to take charge of things when I'm with people	O	O	O
21. I would find it frustrating to sit at a desk all day	O	O	O
22. It is difficult to think up new ways of selling things	O	O	O
23. No job is beneath me	O	O	O
24. I have a very good memory for food package details	O	O	O
25. I do not feel excited by modern day systems technology	O	O	O
26. I dislike having to make snap decisions	O	O	O
27. I take pride in running my own show	O	O	O
28. I like to work regular hours	O	O	O

Figure 6.1 Example of a multiple choice application form
© Sainsbury's Supermarkets Ltd

Making Contact and Filling in the Forms

Figure 6.1 shows part of the Sainsbury's application form, and it's a good example of a multiple choice questionnaire.

If you study the statements in Figure 6.1 you'll see what most of them are getting at, although it depends upon the job you're after as to whether 'agreeing' or 'disagreeing' is the correct answer. However, it's a bit pointless lying and ending up in a job you hate, and anyway, you'll only be caught out at a later stage of the recruitment process, so be honest.

Tips For Filling in Multiple Choice Questions on Application Forms

- With questionnaires designed to be 'marked' by a computer, it's important to complete all the questions or your application could be rejected.

- Follow the instructions to the letter. If you're asked to fill in the circles, don't put ticks in them. If you're asked to use black ink, don't use blue.

General Hints on Filling in Application Forms

Here's how to ensure your form makes a good impression:

- Read the form carefully before you even think about filling it in. Sometimes important instructions appear at the end (on purpose, of course).

- Think about what the employer is looking for. Gather all the information you've discovered about the organization, plus the advertisement, the job specification and applicant profile. Now aim to provide answers that show you as that ideal applicant.

- Use a photocopy of the application form while you're working on your answers. Keep the form itself somewhere safe to ensure it stays clean.

- Use positive, active words to describe your achievements, your capabilities and your interests. Don't be vague.

- Be specific when describing your skills. For example, don't just say you can use a computer. List by name all the packages, programmes and computer languages you are familiar with, and how much experience you have of them.

- Write your answers on a separate piece of paper before you attempt to fill in the form. Don't start until you feel completely satisfied with the answers.

- Check your spelling.

- Don't attempt to type your answers. Application forms are supposed to be handwritten.

- Fill the form in as neatly and legibly as you can. Dirty, messy forms that can't be read easily will be instantly rejected, no matter how brilliant your answers.

- Take a photocopy of the completed form before you send it off, so you remember what you said.

Completing Application Forms on the Spot

At least when you get sent an application form in the post, you've got the luxury of time to prepare your answers. It isn't so easy when one is stuck in front of your nose just before an interview.

If this happens to you, follow the tips given above, paying particular attention to your handwriting and spelling. Carrying a copy of your CV is a good idea, since it will remind you of all those hard-to-remember details about yourself; such as where you went to school and when your birthday is! A good pen and reading glasses if you need them, are also necessities.

Finally

Remember the three main things that impress employers the most about application forms are:

- the instructions have been followed (obvious – but many people don't bother);

- all the questions have been answered fully;

- the form is clean, and the handwriting is neat and legible.

And last, remember that if you are successful, your application form will be kept on file, so be honest. If you lie about academic qualifications, work experience, skills, or even whether you smoke or not – bet on it, you'll be found out.

7 The Telephone Interview

Why Telephone Interviews Exist

Many large companies use a telephone interview as a second stage in the recruitment process. They've already seen your CV or application form, now they use the telephone to check whether you're as good as the 'you' portrayed on paper. If you are, you'll be invited to a face-to-face interview, or possibly some sort of further testing.

Sometimes, the telephone interview is the *first* stage in the process. Unless you make a good impression on the telephone, you won't even be given a chance to fill in an application form.

If you think about it, being interviewed over the telephone is a great idea, not only as far as the employer is concerned, but you too. Many organizations (especially multinational companies) conduct face-to-face interviews at only one or two locations in the country. Imagine spending a day attending an interview hundreds of miles away, only to discover that you would never want to work for them.

Here are the three main reasons why employers conduct interviews on the telephone.

- It's a quick and convenient way to whittle down the number of applicants.

- It's a quick way to check that the applicant possesses the right qualifications.

- It's an essential assessment tool if the job requires a good telephone manner.

In fact, for telephone sales positions, an interview on the telephone may be the only interview you ever get. For this type of work, it's possible to come away from the conversation holding a job offer.

But generally, a telephone interview is just a passport to moving you further along the recruitment process.

When Will it Happen?

The exact time may have been arranged with you in advance, or you may get a call out of the blue. In the latter case, the caller will probably ask you if you have a few minutes to spare. That's when you ask them if they wouldn't mind holding on for a few seconds while you find somewhere quiet to talk.

Do try and find somewhere quiet to talk. Turn the television off, and try to get away from people talking. When you're slightly nervous, trying to concentrate is doubly difficult when you also have to filter out background noise.

How to Prepare

All job-hunters need to be prepared to take telephone calls. The more applications you've made, the more networking you've been doing, the more calls you'll get. So really, you need to be in a constant state of readiness.

The key word is organization. These are the things you must be able to get hold of quickly, when the telephone rings:

- A note book and pen.

- A copy of your CV (if you have more than one version, make sure you know which one you sent to which organization).

- A copy of the application form if you sent one in, so you remember how you answered the questions. You're bound to be asked why you said what you did, or to explain in further detail.

- A copy of the advertisement or the job description if you have it.

- The name of the organization itself, and anything you know about it (which should be quite a lot if you spent even a little time researching).

- Your diary, so you can fix up that all important face-to-face interview.

Of course, if you are serious about landing a job, you'll be applying to many different companies at the same time. This means keeping the details of each application separate. Muddling them up is a recipe for disaster! Plastic folders, which can be bought cheaply from any good stationer, are a perfect way to get yourself organized.

What About the Call Itself?

1. First of all, find out *who* is calling you and from where. That way, you'll be able to grab the right folder immediately.

2. Write the organization's name and the caller's name down on your notepad (don't be shy about asking them to spell their name if you're not sure).

3. Let the caller get on with asking questions, but always ask a few yourself. Remember, even though this is an 'interview', it's also a conversation. That means *both* people have to talk.

4. If you've done any research; let your interviewer know. There's no point having gone to all that bother for nothing. Saying things like, 'I noticed that on your Web site you...', or 'I popped into your local store the other day, and I was

The Telephone Interview

really struck by...' can only impress.

5. If your feel the call is coming to a close, and you're not sure that you've given them enough information, you could always ask, 'Is there anything else I can tell you that would increase my chances further.' Of course, this may mean you'll have to answer another 15 questions, but at least you'll know they're still interested in you.

More Dos and Don'ts

Do:

- be polite and friendly.

- call the interviewer by his/her name every so often; easy when it's written down right in front of you.

- make notes. Anything the caller tells you which you think could be useful ammunition for the next stages of the recruitment process, write it down. The more you know, the more prepared you'll be later on.

Don't:

- interrupt. Wait until it's your turn to speak.

- answer with just 'yes' or 'no' all the time. Try and give a full answer every time; it's the only way to turn an 'interview' into a meaningful conversation.

- get flustered if you don't understand a question. Saying, 'Would you mind repeating that again', or, 'Could you explain what you mean?' is perfectly acceptable.

- mention salary. This is not the time to bring up any of the 'what's in it for me' questions. Remember your objective is to secure a face-to-face meeting.

Body Language

Most of the body language we automatically use when talking to someone face-to-face, is completely missing on the telephone. The person on the other end of the line can't see you, they can only *hear* you.

Of course, this can be an advantage, especially if you've just jumped out of the bath! But there are ways to improve your 'telephone body language'. Here are a few tips:

- Smile. Smiling helps you to relax and makes your voice sound pleasant. You can always tell when someone is smiling. Check it out and see.

- Speak directly into the telephone mouthpiece. It's obvious, but many people hold the telephone so far away, you can't hear a thing they're saying.

- Give the call your complete attention. Don't programme the video, cook the supper or watch a football match at the same time. Your interviewer won't know *what* you're doing, but they *will* know you're not concentrating on them!

And last, a couple of telephone body language don'ts: don't eat anything – eating and chewing noises sound disgusting over the telephone!; and don't smoke – a non-smoker on the other end of the line can always tell.

Your Objective

Throughout the call, whether it lasts for five minutes or a full half hour, you've tried to make the interviewer think, 'This person is worth further consideration'. Your main objective is to secure a face-to-face interview.

If you are successful at doing this, try to find out a little about the interview before you put the telephone down. Who is going to interview you? Bearing in mind you've already been asked quite a lot of questions, are there any other areas they'll want to discuss? The more you can find out now, the more prepared you'll be for that face-to-face meeting.

If the call seems to be drawing to a close and you haven't been asked to come along for a 'proper' interview then you must ask for one. Something like this: 'I'm glad I've had a chance to talk to you. This position really does sound interesting. In fact, from what you've said, it sounds perfect for me and I think I'd be very good at it. I'd really like to come in and meet you; can we fix up a time?' Use your own words, of course, and if possible, give reasons why you think the job sounds like a good one.

Remember, your telephone interviewer is looking for someone who sounds enthusiastic, someone who sounds like they want the job, someone who's taken a little time to find out about the organization, and is capable of asking intelligent questions about the work involved. Just make sure that person is you.

8 The Covering Letter

Every single time you send out your CV by post, you need to send a covering letter of introduction as well.

The purpose of the letter is to:

- persuade the employer to read your CV, and take your application seriously;
- persuade them that you are a suitable candidate;
- say why you want to work for their organization;
- persuade them to offer you an interview.

Persuading the employer to read your CV and take your application seriously, depends largely on the *appearance* of your letter. If it looks good, it will always be read. Conversely, if your letter does not look good, it will be rejected immediately, no matter what's in it, and no matter how great your CV is.

Presentation: the Art of Looking Good

Presentation is the single most important thing to determine whether your letter is picked up or thrown out. Here are some sensible, no nonsense tips for making your letter look good enough to read.

- *Size?* Use A4 size paper (21 cm wide x 29.7 cm deep). This is the accepted size paper for business letters. Your covering letter is also a business letter.

The Covering Letter

- *Plain or lined?*: Use plain paper, lined paper isn't businesslike. Fancy borders and background pictures are also out.

- *Colour?* Use white or cream coloured paper. If your budget will stretch to a watermarked paper, even better.

- *Weight?* Use paper that is around 90 to 100 gsm. Anything less will feel too flimsy, anything much heavier will feel too thick.

- *Appearance?* Obviously, it should be clean. Not just clean, pristine.

- *Hand written or word-processed?* Word-processed if possible. Only send hand-written letters if specifically requested, or if your handwriting is exquisite *and* very easy to read.

- *What font?* Use a businesslike, unfussy style. Times New Roman is one suggestion, but only a suggestion. Save the fun stuff for birthday cards.

- *What size font?* Using Times New Roman as a guide, 12 point. Anything smaller could be difficult to read.

- *Top copy?* Definitely. Never send photocopied letters.

Remember, your covering letter does not have to be a million times better than the rest to be picked up and read. As with CVs, the vast majority of letters will be poorly presented, and many will be appalling.

If you follow these basic rules, *your* covering letter will look businesslike and well presented. For even more detail read Chapters 9 and 10, since much of the advice on CVs applies to covering letters too.

Landing Your First Job

Ms L Ford
Recruitment Manager
Human Resources Department
Finer Foods Ltd
Holmer Industrial Park
London SW9 5YH   10 March 1999

Dear Ms Ford

Re: Assistant Press Officer

I am writing in response to your advertisement in today's *Daily Telegraph* for the above position. I regularly purchase your products and have been particularly impressed by the quality of your frogs' legs.

As you can see from my Curriculum Vitae, I already have considerable experience of press officer work, being responsible for all student union press contacts from 1997 to the present time. I have also been involved in press release production and distribution for every major university event.

My work experience during holidays has also helped me develop a number of the skills mentioned in your advertisement, particularly team working and organizing my schedule around tight deadlines. I am confident I could bring ideas and enthusiasm to the job.

I would very much welcome the opportunity of an interview to discuss this further.

Yours sincerely

Jack Daniels

16 Wilson Street
London EC2 5PY
Tel 0181 111 1234
Jack@madeup.net

Enclosure: Curriculum Vitae

Figure 8.1: Example of a covering letter

Layout

Your covering letter should take up no more than one page. Always aim to position the text so as to give a pleasing appearance. Don't squash it all up at the top and leave a big gap at the bottom. Aim for balance.

If you look at Figure 8.1 you will see how every line (with the exception of the date) begins at the left hand margin. This is the way most business letters are written and your covering letter is a business letter too.

Leave around six or seven lines blank, at the top of the page. Not only will this give a balanced look, the name and address of the person you're writing to will appear in the correct position for a window envelope. If you're not used to writing business letters, experiment until you get it right.

The Content of Your Covering Letter

To Whom are You Writing?

Most job advertisements tell you who to contact. If there's no name (or you're writing in on spec) you'll have to ring up and ask. While you're on the telephone, check the spelling of the name. You don't want to antagonize the recruiter the moment they pick up your letter.

Assuming you know who to write to, begin your letter with 'Dear', and then the person's name. When you start a letter off this way, always end with, 'Yours sincerely'.

If you really cannot get a name, you'll have to begin your letter with, 'Dear Sir or Madam'. In this case, the letter must end, 'Yours faithfully'.

The Heading

This informs the reader which job you are applying for. In case you think it's obvious, sometimes it isn't.

For a start they might be advertising more than one job. Second, recruitment advertising is expensive. Organizations need to know which method produces the best quality response, so that they can target their advertising as effectively as possible. Use **bold** for this line.

The First Paragraph

Here's where you introduce yourself and say why you are writing to them and why you want to work for them. The text I've used is a bit jokey – but I'm trying to make a point. It's good to demonstrate that you have researched their company and that you liked what you saw.

The Second Paragraph

This is where you start selling yourself. Pick out the salient points from your CV and include them here. Aim to make the person reading your letter think, 'This sounds good. He might be the one'.

Think about what the organization is looking for in the successful candidate. Re-read the advertisement. Study the job description and 'person specification' if there is one, and any other information you discovered during your research. What can you offer to make you the right choice?

The Third Paragraph

Can you think of anything else that would persuade the reader to consider you? Don't forget to mention your leisure interests or your academic course work, if they demonstrate your suitability. Previous work and voluntary activities can also be included, but don't go too over the top. The covering letter is supposed to interest the reader in your CV, and that's where most of the detail should go. Besides, you have to stick to one page. Using Times New Roman in 12 point only allows you around 250 words for the main body of the letter.

The Last Paragraph

Let the employer know that you would welcome the opportunity of an interview (and when you are available if your time is limited). Make sure you use a phrase that gives you the option to make contact. If you say, 'I look forward to hearing from you', you've handed over all that responsibility to them.

Also, never be apologetic. A phrase such as, 'I really would be extremely grateful', just makes you sound desperate and will turn an employer off immediately. Aim to sound confident but not conceited.

The Ending

After the 'Yours sincerely', you need to leave a gap in which to sign your name. Then print your name. Current thinking is not to use your title, Mrs or Miss or Mr, because it could appear too formal. Just print your first name and surname, as per the example letter.

Your Contact Details

There's no point writing a really good letter and forgetting to put your address and contact details on it – and you'd be surprised how many people do just that. Even though your address and telephone number are in your CV, they still need to be on the letter. If you have an e-mail address, include it too.

If you don't have enough room at the bottom, position your personal contact details opposite the name and address of the company to which you are writing.

Anything Else?

Assuming you are enclosing a CV, write 'Enclosure: Curriculum Vitae' on the very bottom line. And don't forget to sign and date your letter.

Do Application Forms Need Covering Letters?

Opinion is divided on this, but personally I believe the answer is yes, out of courtesy if nothing else. You still need to introduce yourself, and explain why you're sending the form. Application forms can also be pretty basic. They don't always ask the right questions. The only place to say the things you really want to say is in a letter.

Words of Warning

Make sure that whatever you put in your covering letter appears in your CV or application form, too. Employers are well used to letters stating that the candidate is a 'great salesperson' only to find there isn't a shred of evidence in the CV to substantiate the claim.

Being 'Clever'

Although this little piece of advice appears earlier in the book, I wanted to repeat it again here, simply because it's so important. There are quite a lot of people out there who, when asked to send a covering letter, send instead their name and address and a little note saying something like 'I'm brilliant – contact me and find out!' and nothing else. Unsurprisingly, this will result in instant rejection.

Postage

An obvious point perhaps, but this applies to any material you send out, whether it's in response to an advertisement or on spec. Make sure you put the correct postage on the envelope. If you're not sure, get it weighed at the post office.

Finally

Employers know that a good covering letter takes time and effort to produce. The best covering letters are ones that are tailored to the employer's requirements.

Unfortunately this means you have to write a different letter every single time you apply for a job (although if you're applying for very similar jobs, you might not have to do a complete rewrite every time). But it's still worth the effort.

9 Preparing Your CV: Style and Format

I once received a letter from someone who said it was unfair to offer an interview to only a small percentage of people applying for a job. Why couldn't everyone be interviewed? The fact is, your CV is your first interview.

No employer wants to interview full time. It's very tiring and extremely costly, not to mention confusing (see Chapter 17). Instead, the first thing they do is simply pick out the most presentable looking CVs, and discard the rest.

It doesn't matter what your CV actually says at this stage. It doesn't matter how great you'd be if you got the job. The only thing that matters to the employer is what your CV *actually looks like*. And that is what this chapter is about – making your CV look good.

The General Appearance of Your CV

The good news is that your CV doesn't have to be a million times better than the rest to be picked out. The truth is, for every job advertised, the vast majority of CVs received will be badly presented. Following the basic advice in this chapter will put your CV into the top 10 per cent immediately.

Make it Look Professional

Aim to make your CV look businesslike and professional, no matter what the job. It goes without saying that the document

Preparing Your CV: Style and Format

should be clean, but you'd be surprised how many people send out scruffy little bits of paper covered in coffee stains.

Take a look at your current CV. Does it look good, or does it look a bit of a mess? Perhaps now is the time to do something about it. Here are the main ways to ensure your CV looks good:

- *Paper size?* Use A4 size paper (21 cm wide x 29.7 cm deep). This is the accepted size paper for CVs.

- *Plain or lined?* Use plain paper. Lined paper isn't businesslike. Do not incorporate fancy borders and background pictures.

- *Colour?* Use only white or cream coloured paper.

- *Weight?* Use paper that is around 90 to 100 gsm. Anything less will feel too flimsy, anything much heavier will feel too thick. If your budget will stretch to a watermarked paper, even better.

- *Appearance?* It should be spotless.

- *What font?* Use a businesslike, unfussy style. Times New Roman is one suggestion.

- *What size font?* Using Times New Roman as a guide, 12 point, for the main body copy. Anything smaller could be difficult to read. You can use a slightly larger size for headings, but bold can be just as effective.

- *Colour?* If you are using a colour printer resist the temptation to use lots of colour. Plain black ink is best, although a little grey shading here and there looks good. See the example CVs in the next chapter.

Should Your CV Be Hand-written?

The answer to this question is a resounding 'no'. Here are a few reasons why you should not hand-write your CVs:

- it looks old-fashioned;

- it could make you appear amateurish;

- it could make the person reading it think you have no experience of using a computer;

- it could be difficult to read.

On this last point, even the most stylish hand-writing can be illegible. Hand-written CVs are more likely to be discarded in favour of nicely printed ones, so however beautiful your writing, don't do it.

> **Note:** the advice given on this subject under 'The Covering Letter' in Chapter 8 is slightly different.

Should Your CV Be Typed?

By 'typed' I mean using a typewriter. The answer to this question is no. Here are a few reasons why you should not type your CV:

- text which is 'typed' does not look businesslike;

- it could make you appear amateurish;

- it could make the person reading it think you have no experience of using a computer;

- it is difficult to type pages of text without making mistakes. A CV with even one spot of correction fluid on it will look a mess.

Should Your CV Be Printed?

The answer here, of course, is 'yes'. You want your CV to look businesslike, and all business letters are printed. Therefore your CV has to be printed. But what if you don't have access to a computer and printer? Here are a few ideas:

- Ask a friend if you can use his or her computer and printer.

- Go to a high street printing shop (with your previously prepared CV) and ask them to get it printed up for you.

- Use the computer and printer at your school/college or university.

- Use the computer and printer in the local library.

There is no excuse for not printing your CV. Besides, if your CV is prepared on a computer, printing out multiple copies or tailoring each one to a specific employer's requirements should be relatively easy.

> **Tip:** Every time you send your CV out, send a top copy, fresh off the printer. Never send photocopies.

How Long Should a CV Be?

Aim to produce one page of text, two at the very most. Sending out 10 pages will prove counter-productive. No one will read it.

Print your CV on just one side of the A4 sheet. If your CV is two pages long, you'll need two pieces of paper. Ensure your name and telephone number appear on each sheet.

Keeping Your Document Together

If you send out more than one sheet, you will have to decide how to fix them together. Acceptable methods of keeping your CV together are using either staples (stapling the document once neatly in the top left-hand corner), or document wallets.

Document wallets are clear folders which can be bought quite cheaply from all good stationers. Not only do they keep your document together, they keep it clean too.

Unacceptable methods of keeping your CV together are using either paper-clips, which have a tendency to work loose, or using nothing. Employers, interviewers and personnel staff are as careless as the rest of us and if your CV isn't fixed together somehow, some of it will get lost.

> **Tip:** Don't fix your covering letter to your CV. Put it in the same envelope, of course, but separately.

A Final Note on Style and Format

Try a variety of styles and sizes, until you get a lookwith which you feel comfortable. If in doubt, ask friends and relations for their feedback. The next chapter covers the content of your CV, and also layout, since this is easier to illustrate than write about.

10 Preparing Your CV: The Content

Figures 10.1 and 10.2 show two different example CVs. Both of them belong to real people (with just a few identifying details changed) and both CVs have recently proved very successful indeed. If you want to, model your own CV on the one you like best.

> **Note:** Don't forget the virtual CV in Chapter 3 – you can also see it in full colour on my own net site at http://www.shavick.com

Personal Details

Personal details are your name, address, contact telephone number, e-mail address, age, and status (whether you're married or not).

All these details usually go at the top of the CV. Your name and telephone number should also appear on the following sheets (if your CV is more than one page) in case they become separated from one another.

Landing Your First Job

12 Hillside Close
Crouch End
London N8 3TR

0181 123 4567 (Home)

Alex Jones

Personal Information
- Marital status: Single
- Nationality: British
- Age: 22

Education and Qualifications

1995 – 98
Gonville and Caius College, Cambridge
- Maths Tripos Part II: II-1 (BA Hons)
- Maths Tripos Part III: Pass

1988 – 1994
The Haberdashers' Aske's School, Elstree
- GCSEs: 9 As, 1 B
- A levels: Maths (A), Further Maths (A) Physics (B)

Work Experience

1996 and 1997
Touche Ross   Holiday work in accountancy.

1994 – 95
Compusoft   Gap year work in programming.

IT Experience
- Environments: Windows NT, Windows 95, OS/2 Unix (½ years)
- Languages: Visual C++, Pascal, Basic

Interests and Activities
- Sport: Football
  Basketball (College captain)
  Squash
  Tennis (College 2nd team captain)
  Fitness
- Music: I play piano and guitar
- Leisure: Bridge (College captain)
  Reading
- Other: Conversational French and German
  Full clean driving licence.

Figures 10.1 and 10.2: Two Sample CVs

Preparing Your CV: The Content

JOANNE GREEN

Current address:	228 Cambridge Road, Cambridge CB2 4PY
Current e-mail:	Joanne@madeup.net
Tel:	01223 123456
Nationality:	British Date of Birth: 21.04.76 Status: Single

EDUCATION

1995 – 99 King's College, Cambridge University
BA Honours Degree in Modern Language – Italian and French (language, literature and film)

Part II (Finals)	Ist Class
Part I French	Ist Class
Part I Italian	2:1

1989 – 95 Hendon Comprehensive School, London
GCSE   9 at A grade, including Maths, German and French
A level   English (A), French (A), History (A)

EXPERIENCE
Arts Production

March 1997 – 98   Postproducer assistant in post-production company, Special Effects Ltd; coordination of post-production on full commercial productions and of foreign language commercial versions. Position includes: budgeting, scheduling, booking facility houses, liaising with clients and production companies.

1996 – 97   TV production, documentary department of Cambridge student television; produced 'Rough Guide' to Cambridge.

1996 – 97   Film review contributor, *Cambridge Student News*.

1995 – 96   Editor/writer, King's College student magazine.

Arts Activities

1996   Member of Bologna University Choir, Italy.
1996   Sang with King's College Chapel Choir.
1993   Member of chorus in two English National Opera productions at the London Coliseum.

Organization

1996 – 97   Student representative for Cambridge University Contemporary Cinema course.
1995 – 96   Captain, college badminton team.
1993 – 95   Secretary, school debating society.
1992   Founding member, history society.
         Organizer, fund-raising event (Kampuchean Aid Appeal).

Research

1998 – 99   First class distinction for final year dissertation, *The Imprisoning Gaze: A Study of Three Works* by Luigi Pirandello.

Communication

1996   Freelance translation/interpreting (Italian/English); private English teaching, Bologna Italy 1996 Translation (Italian/English), Bologna, Italy.

ADDITIONAL SKILLS

Languages: Fluent French, Italian, and Danish. I have recently started learning Spanish.

INTERESTS

Cinema, literature, history, hiking. I am a member of the *Cinematography Mailing List* and the *Telecine Internet Group*, and read both on a daily basis.

Name

Obviously your name has to go on the CV, but how to write it? 'John Smith', this is fine, or 'J Smith', this is rather impersonal, plus it doesn't tell an employer whether 'J Smith' is male or female. Do not write 'John Smith (male)'.

You would be amazed how many people announce their gender by writing, 'male' or 'female' after their names. It looks ridiculous. In most cases, anybody reading your CV will know whether you are male or female just by looking at your name. If there is any ambiguity about it, include your middle name or a photograph just to make things crystal clear. Or don't worry about it.

On the subject of names, use your real name not your nickname.

Address

Obviously you need to give your address on your CV, since hopefully, employers will be writing to you with job offers. If you are working abroad through a gap year, make sure you give an address where there is someone you can rely on to forward your post on to you. This is where e-mail is invaluable, since you can access your post from anywhere in the world. So together with your address, print your current e-mail address too.

Telephone Numbers

You can give fax numbers and e-mail addresses, but when they're trying to get in touch, employers generally prefer the good old-fashioned telephone. Make sure there's somebody around to take the call; an unmanned telephone is very off-putting to an employer. If they can't reach you, they'll just try the next candidate instead.

If you do have someone to answer the telephone for you, consider the impression they might make. Will they be friendly? Will they take a message? And have you told them that potential employers might call you up? Making sure your message-taker is well prepared and sensible. After all, you don't want them to say something like, 'Oh he's down the pub today, bunking off college.'

If you can only be contacted at certain times of the day, say so. Print, after the number, 'After 6 pm weekdays', or whenever you are available. Employers are used to contacting people in the evening, but if you can give a daytime telephone number, so much the better.

One more point; in the future, when you're working, never put your current employer's telephone number on your CV.

Photographs

There are arguments for and against sending a photograph. If you have a pleasing photo of yourself that you'd like to attach to your CV, then by all means do so. Including a photo of yourself makes the whole document much more personal. It's also quite unusual for candidates to send a photo, so you'll stand out from the crowd.

If you do decide to send a photo, staple it to the front of your CV in a prominent position (probably best top right) but not so as to obscure any text. For the most professional feel, scan the photo in so it becomes part of the document.

Whatever you do, make sure the picture is flattering, a smiling head and shoulders shot would do nicely.

Sometimes people are reluctant to send photographs because they think an employer might reject them through prejudice, or a predetermined idea of what the successful candidate will look like. If this is true of the organization you are applying to perhaps you'd be better off not working for them.

If you feel comfortable sending a photograph, do so. If not, forget about it.

Status

What to put down as your 'status' is also a difficult one. Status means whether you are married or not. You are either single, married or divorced (although you could truthfully say you are single if you've been divorced).

Although we live in a liberal society, people do have their prejudices. For instance, if you say you're divorced with three young children, it could be interpreted as showing a lack of commitment.

So decide what you feel most comfortable telling an employer and stick to that. One word of warning: if your CV doesn't make your 'status' clear, you could be asked about it at interview.

Date of Birth or Age, or Both?

It doesn't matter whether you print your date of birth or your age, but it isn't necessary to put both in. If you do print your age, remember to update your CV each year.

Education

Follow the layout in whichever one of the examples you prefer, Figure 10.1 or 10.2. Examination grades, if good, should be given, as can expected results if you haven't yet graduated. Details of your academic achievements should be included, but don't send actual certificates. A list of them is all you need.

Don't be tempted to lie about grades, or even the subjects you studied. It isn't worth it. Once you've been offered a job you may have to provide evidence of your educational qualifications. If you've failed an exam, just don't mention it.

Work Experience

This is where you score if you've worked throughout a gap year, or during the holidays. Any part-time or temporary work will also demonstrate that you have the ability and motivation to do something constructive rather than laze around. Work experience, and the more of it the better, shows you understand the 'work ethic' that is valued so highly by employers, the ability to get up every morning and go to work.

Preparing Your CV: The Content

Putting in some information about any work experience you've had also gives an employer something to talk about during an interview. Although you don't need to go into minute detail about what you did during that three-week work placement, some information would be a good idea, especially if the job you're after is in the same industry. Your covering letter is a better place to go into detail. Furthermore, it can be tailored to every single application you make – something that isn't always possible to do with a CV.

> **Note:** Once you have permanent work experience under your belt, you will have to allocate a lot more space on your CV for it.

If you look at the two sample CVs shown in Figures 10.1 and 10.2, and the virtual CV in Chapter 3, you will see that very little information is given about temporary and part-time work experience, although from the overall amount of information given, an employer will see straight away that these people are energetic, motivated, intelligent, enterprising, and doing everything possible to expand their knowledge and experience for their chosen careers.

Other Skills

Information which does not readily fall into 'work experience', and isn't a leisure interest, can be grouped together under a heading like 'additional skills'. The sort of things which would be included here would be:

- driving licence – perhaps you could mention that you have your own car;
- language skills – detailing which languages;

- IT skills – the computer packages and languages with which you are familiar.

Any positive information about yourself and your abilities, which have not already been covered, can go under this heading. You may not need IT skills or a foreign language for the job you want, but if you possess them, put them in.

Interests and Activities

A lot is written about hobbies, which ones are 'good' ones to have, and which ones might put an employer off. The truth is that employers do not have time to consider your hobbies in any depth when they are sifting through job applications. But at the interview stage, it's a different story. You are more likely to be asked about your leisure interests here because it's often the way interviewers break the ice. They want to help you relax and open up, create a rapport with you. If you are a graduate, or fresh out of school, you won't have years of job experience behind you. The interviewer has to ask you about something. If there is very little employment history to discuss, leisure interests are the next best thing.

So Are There Any 'Good' Interests to Have?

The best interests to have are ones that demonstrate to the employer that you are the right person for the job. For instance:

- If you want to work in the computer industry and have always written your own computer games – say so.

- If you want to work in catering and have always created great birthday cakes for your friends and family – say so.

- If you want to work in the caring sector and regularly shop for your elderly neighbours – say so.

■ If you want to work with animals and spend your spare time helping out at the animal rescue centre – say so.

Employers are impressed by candidates who show an interest in their field. They know that if you are *interested* in your job, you will *enjoy* your job and if you enjoy your job you'll be good at it.

What if Your Leisure Activities Are Not Related to the Job?

Think about the things you do with your spare time. Is there anything you can say which will impress an employer? What about these suggestions: Are you a member of a team; any kind of team will do. Demonstrating the ability to work with other people is impressive, especially if you talk about it with enthusiasm. Do you spend time organizing anything; the student magazine, or a club or college society for instance. Any evidence of organizational abilities goes down well. If you attend a club but never get involved with any of the organization, perhaps now is a good time to start.

Why You Must Be Honest About Your Interests

Thinking up worthy leisure time activities is one thing, answering questions about them is quite another! And you *will* be asked. For example, if you state 'reading' as one of your interests, the interviewer is bound to ask, 'What's the last book you read?' or 'Who is your favourite author?'

If you state 'going to the theatre', you'll be asked what you've seen recently. And if you've put down 'tap dancing', who knows – you might be asked to give a demonstration!

Salary Requirements

Most job advertisements do not include salary details because organizations generally prefer to wait until they've found a promising candidate before bringing up the subject. It is a good idea to do a little research on salaries (lots of ideas in Chapter 1) simply so you know the current rate for the job. If you are at the very beginning of your career, you'll need to know entry level salaries too.

As far as your CV is concerned, common wisdom is not to state your salary requirements on it. Certainly if you do it takes away all your negotiating power later on. The only time you should mention salary is when you reply to an advertisement that requests you 'state your salary expectations'. In this case, be vague and say, 'In the region of...' and then state the general salary range according to your research.

References

If you haven't worked before you should still have plenty of people to use as referees, such as your college professors and lecturers. Other people who have known you for a long time, such as relatives or friends of your parents (preferably in a professional occupation) will also suffice. With part-time, holiday, or voluntary work experience under your belt, the people who employed you would also make a good choice.

It isn't necessary to give the names of referees in your CV, but if you do, choose two, or possibly three people from different areas of your life, ie not all from college. Always make sure you:

- ask their permission first;

- give them a copy of your CV;

- tell them who you are applying to.

You can even write down the sort of things you want them to say, and hopefully they will!

> **Tip:** Never send written references with your CV, it will make you look desperate. If your new employer wants references, you'll be asked to provide them once you've been offered the job.

Word of Warning

Don't ask any of your referees to lie about you. It's possible to be sued for providing misleading or completely untruthful information in a reference.

Being Truthful

With application forms, you have to answer the questions the organization wants answered. With a CV, *you* decide what to include and what to leave out. But although you naturally want to paint the best picture possible, telling downright lies is always a bad idea. And why? You'll be found out. Here's how:

- At an interview, your CV gives the interviewer something to ask questions about. If you're falsely claiming experience of XYZ, it will be quite obvious that you don't know what you're talking about.

- It's easy to forget what you've written on your CV when confronted with an application form during the course of an interview. Any discrepancy between the two and alarm bells start ringing for the employer.

- If you're offered the job, your new employer may take up references. Some of the information on your CV could be checked out then. You don't want to go through the whole process only to have someone say, 'That's strange. I had no idea he passed so many A levels.'

So it isn't a good idea to lie, and it isn't necessary anyway.

CV Writing Services

Many people think that it is perfectly acceptable to go to a 'CV writing service' and have a complete stranger compose their CV for them. Why do they do it?

Perhaps they think a CV writing service will do a better job than they can. Perhaps they simply can't be bothered to do it themselves. The truth is that most employers can spot a CV or a covering letter written by 'CV writing service' a mile off. Often they are:

- printed on fancy paper, often a coloured paper with a fussy border;

- full of highly decorative font styles and even pretty little pictures;

- written in the third person, eg 'He is a fantastic salesman'. 'She is a good organizer'.

None of the above will impress an employer. They'll think the beautiful borders and fancy fonts are cute, but surely you can't be serious? They'll think you can't be bothered to write your own CV. Even worse, they'll think that you are incapable of doing it. They'll know, by the use of the third person pronoun, that you didn't write the words.

This apparent inability to compose your own CV is especially off-putting to employers who are trying to fill positions involving any element of customer contact. They'll think, 'If she isn't capable of representing herself, how on earth will she represent my company?'

So take the time to compose your own CV and don't entrust the job to a stranger, especially one who assures you that fancy borders and coloured paper will 'get you noticed'. It will, but not the way you want it to.

Tip: It's fine to use a print shop to print up your CV if you don't have access to a computer and printer. Just make sure you write the words and the finished article looks businesslike. Always keep a copy of your CV. If you change it, make sure you know which version you've sent to which organization.

11 Applying for Jobs 'On Spec'

Why compete with other candidates chasing advertised positions when you could go for a job where there is only one candidate? You!

'On spec' means approaching an organization for a job using your own initiative, without responding to an advertisement. It isn't the only option for finding a job, but it is an extremely good one.

What Size of Organization to Target

Large organizations are recruiting all the time. Some of them have up to 80 per cent turnover of staff per annum! This means that there are always job opportunities available, and many of them will never be advertised. But they exist.

Smaller organizations employ fewer people, but most of them think about staffing problems all the time. They also have to replace staff who are leaving or not working out. They also need more people when business is booming or new products are launched.

Which is a Better Bet?

Both large and small organizations are worth approaching. The main difference is that with a small one, it's easier to get to the decision maker. If you approach a small company, chances are that you'll be talking to the proprietor, a director, or a senior manager within a few minutes.

Applying for Jobs 'On Spec'

The larger the organization, the more layers of management you'll have to go through. Large organizations tend to have personnel/human resource departments which filter potential new recruits without having any actual decision-making powers, and it's the decision maker you need to be selling your skills to. Having said that, personnel staff can often be extremely helpful and even the key to achieving the job offer you want.

Do Organizations Take on Staff They're Not Looking For?

Yes they do, all the time. If they like you and can see you've got something to offer, then you're *definitely* in with a chance. As one employer put it, 'If somebody approaches us out of the blue; if we think they're worth having, even if there's nothing available immediately we start thinking about creating a role for them.'

Where to Start

Since there are literally hundreds of thousands of organizations you could approach, you must find some way of narrowing down the list and targeting the ones with which you have the best chance of success.

Draw up a list of the skills, the knowledge, the qualifications and the experience you have. Targeting organizations which will be interested in the abilities you possess, is the best place to start.

Then think about what you want. At the beginning of Chapter 1 there is a section devoted entirely to imagining your ideal job. What *do* you want to do? Where *do* you want to work? Who *do* you want to work with? It's easier to track down your ideal job if you know what you're looking for.

Armed with the knowledge of what you have to offer, and with a clearer idea of for whom and where you want to work, it's time to identify your targets. Get their names and addresses from:

Landing Your First Job

- the trade association or society for the profession you're interested in. They'll have lists of member companies, and will definitely be able to supply you with addresses and telephone numbers (and possibly contact names too);

- employer files at your careers service;

- business directories, eg *Yellow Pages*, *Business Pages* and *Kompass*;

- libraries, local authority careers services and the local Chamber of Commerce;

- the Internet.

Tip: To get the name and address of a specific trade association, ask your careers service or read careers books. Also see Further Reading at the back of the book for suggestions.

If the location of your job is important, local newspapers are an excellent place to find potential employers. Why not start with the companies which advertise regularly, not just for staff, but products and services too.

Scan the papers to find out which organizations are expanding, launching new products, winning new contracts or relocating. All of them could be looking for more people.

Preparation

Once you have a list of possible 'targets', a little more research is in order. The very first question they're going to ask is, 'Why do you want to work for us?' and if you haven't a clue what they do, you won't be able to answer the question. Find out more about them by:

- going along to their nearest branch (if they have one) and having a look round.

- finding out about the product or service they offer. Can you buy it, or try it?

- do they have any literature you can look at, eg leaflets, catalogues or a staff magazine you can subscribe to? Ring up and ask.

- do they have a Web site you can look at? If the address isn't on their literature, ring up and ask.

- what about the organization's advertising? Where do they advertise? What do they advertise? Do they maintain a high profile? What sort of image are they trying to promote?

Even if they ask why you want the information, follow the suggestion in Chapter 5 and tell the truth. Say, 'I'm interested in working for you, and I'd like to find out more before I get in touch officially.'

What About the Actual Approach?

There are several different ways to approach an organization on spec. They are:

- physically knocking on the door;
- telephoning;
- making your approach in writing;
- sending an e-mail.

Physically Knocking on the Door

One way of finding out if there are any vacancies in an organization is to go along to their premises and ask. If the organization has retail outlets into which any member of the public can walk – why not make your approach this way. Once you're there, you might find leaflets about working for them, or job ads in the window (and not necessarily junior jobs either). If not you'll have to ask.

It might feel highly embarrassing, asking to see the person who deals with staff vacancies, but the worst thing that can possibly happen is that they say, 'No, sorry we haven't any vacancies right now.'

Even if that does happen, you can still ask where they do advertise when they need staff. Try and find out whether there's anyone you can write to who will keep your details on file for future reference.

Other, more likely reactions are:

- 'Send us a letter and CV, and we'll get back to you.' Make sure you do. Before you leave, thank the person you saw, and find out exactly who to write to.

- 'Contact our head office, they deal with staff recruitment.' Before you leave, get the details. Can they give you a name? Personal contacts are valuable.

- 'We haven't got anything at the moment, but try again in a month's time.' Engage them in conversation. Do they know of a vacancy coming up? Will it be advertised, and if so, where? Can you write to them in the meantime?

Whatever happens, it's worth a go. They might say, 'Actually we do have a vacancy at the moment, have you got time to discuss it now?' in which case you'll have to go straight into interview mode.

Tips For Making Your Approach In Person

- Dress smartly and make sure you look clean and presentable.

- Act in a professional manner just as you would for a pre-arranged interview.

- Take along copies of your CV, just in case.

- Take a notebook and pen to write down contact names and telephone numbers.

Telephoning

This is the quickest and easiest way to approach companies on spec. But who do you ask for, and what do you say?

Who to Ask For

A lot depends upon the job you're after, and the skills you possess. If you're interested in:

- finance – ask for the financial director, or the chief accountant;

- sales – ask for the sales director;

- administration – ask for the office manager;

- if you're an electronics engineer – ask for the chief engineer.

Go for the person most likely to be your immediate boss if you were hired, rather than the chief executive or human resources manager.

> **Tip:** It's much easier to get your call put through if you can ask for a specific person by name. If you don't already know the name of the right person, ring up and ask the receptionist. Then you can ask to be put through to them. If you need to do a bit of thinking first, hang up and ring back when you're ready.

Shouldn't I Ask For the Personnel Department First?

No. First of all, most small companies don't have a personnel department. Individual managers, or directors will make hiring decisions and they are the people you need to speak to.

When you're dealing with an organization that does have one, it's still better to speak to whoever would be your immediate boss first. They may well refer you back to personnel, but if you *start* with personnel you're unlikely to be referred to the finance director, or the chief engineer.

What to Say First

Once you're through to the decision maker (you may have to explain the reason for your call to their assistant or secretary as well), introduce yourself, and then come straight to the point. 'I'm an experienced astronaut and as soon as I read in the press that you were planning a mission to Mars, I had to call you straight away.'

Rather a silly example, but the point is that you need to explain straight away why you are calling them for a job. It isn't really enough to say: 'I'm calling to see whether you have any job vacancies at the moment.' You need to give them a reason to be interested in you.

If you've followed the suggestions in this chapter, you'll have targeted this particular organization because you feel they'll be interested in the skills you have and you feel they can offer you what you want. If you've also researched the company and know what they do, it shouldn't be too difficult to make your opening sentence a good one.

Applying for Jobs 'On Spec'

> **Tip:** Write your opening sentence on a piece of paper and keep it in front of you throughout the call. Write down the name of the person you're calling too. Now you won't forget why you're calling or who you're talking to; both quite possible when you're feeling under stress.

What to Say Next

Once you've spoken your opening lines, keep quiet and wait for a reply. Although there are books that recommend preparing an entire script, this really isn't feasible. There is simply no way of predicting what the person on the other end of the line is going to say next.

When they do start talking, aim to keep the conversation going. Be prepared to answer questions. You're bound to be asked *why* you want to work for that particular organization as well as what qualities you have to offer. Obviously, if you've previously taken the time to find out a little about the organization, and you've thought about what it is that *you* want, you'll be able to give convincing and truthful answers.

Some tips for getting the most out of your conversation:

- smile – it shows in your voice;

- sound enthusiastic;

- be polite and friendly;

- keep a notepad handy to jot down what you're told, be it to send your CV, contact Head Office, ring back in a month's time, or whatever.

Read more about telephone techniques in Chapter 7.

What to Expect

If the conversation goes well, you should aim to set up a meeting so you can continue the discussion face-to-face. That's the only way you're going to be offered a job; you're very unlikely to be offered anything during the first telephone call.

So if the call goes well, ask for a meeting. 'Can I come in and see you?' or, 'I'd really like to come in and continue this discussion' or, 'When can we meet?' If you're really lucky, they'll make the suggestion. Keep your diary handy, and if you do get invited along for an interview, make sure you're clear about the date, time and correct address *before* you hang up.

The most likely response, even if they are extremely interested in you, will be a request for you to write in. Most organizations, large and small, will expect you to send a letter and a CV before they'll consider offering an interview.

If this is the outcome of your telephone conversation, read Chapters 8, 9 and 10. The advantage of having made the call is that now:

- you have a specific person to write to;

- you can start the letter off on a very personal note, 'When we spoke on the telephone yesterday, you asked me to send you a copy of my CV';

- they'll be waiting for your letter.

How to Keep Your Foot in the Door

If the person you spoke to sounded even the slightest bit interested in you, but doesn't have any vacancies at the moment, here are some suggestions for keeping the door open. Ask whether you can send your CV in anyway and would they hold it on file in case anything suitable does come up? Say something like, 'Would you mind if I called you again, say in a month's time?' Who can object to that? You'll certainly appear enthusiastic, and it may lead to a job opening.

Whatever happens, if you say you are going to ring back or write in, make sure you do. When it comes to job-hunting, always keep your promises.

Writing

If you decide that you'd rather write a letter first, then all the suggestions discussed in Chapter 8 still hold. The art of writing letters to prospective employers is the same whether or not you're responding to an advertisement or not. The main difference is that because you are writing 'out of the blue', you won't be able to head your letter up with a specific job title. Instead you'll have to attract the reader's attention by coming to the point quickly. Figure 11.1 shows an example of a speculative letter.

Tips on Writing Speculative Letters

- Always write to a specific person. Ideally it should be the person who would be your immediate boss if you were hired. If you don't know who this is, ring up and ask. While you're on the telephone, check the spelling of their name and their official title.

- Make it easy for the organization to contact you. Put your address, telephone number and e-mail address on the letter, not just in your CV.

- Remember that unless your letter looks presentable, it will not be taken seriously.

- In the letter itself: introduce yourself, indicate the sort of work you're looking for, mention your most relevant selling points and don't forget to say why you're interested in *them*. End on a positive note, which allows you to contact them. Writing 'I look forward to hearing from you', only allows them to take the initiative.

- Accept the fact that you will have to write a lot of letters to obtain even one positive response. But don't give up, this approach is definitely worthwhile.

- Always follow up your letter with a telephone call, around a week later. Just because you haven't received an immediate response doesn't mean they're not interested. They could simply be waiting for you to contact them.

Sending an E-mail

Practically every organization in commerce or industry uses e-mail, even if they don't have a proper Web site. Although using the Internet is covered in detail in Chapter 3, using e-mail to apply for jobs on spec is very effective.

You still need to find out who to approach; usually by telephoning the company. But this time, instead of asking to be put through, ask for the person's e-mail address. If the receptionist doesn't know, you will have to ask the person directly. You don't need to get into a conversation if you don't want to; just introduce yourself and then say something like, 'Would it be possible to have your e-mail address? I'd like to send you a message?'

Then you just send them your on spec letter (with your CV) via e-mail.

Tips For Sending Speculative Letters Via E-mail

As above, make sure you're e-mailing the person who would be your immediate boss if you were hired.

The language of e-mail is more casual than it is for business letters. Although you could use the same example letter as shown in Figure 11.1, you won't need the company address (just the e-mail address), and you can dispense with the 'Yours sincerely' altogether and use 'Best regards', instead.

Any response is likely to be sent back to you via e-mail so keep logging on. If there is no response, try another message, or alternatively use the telephone.

Applying for Jobs 'On Spec'

> Mrs J Smith, Director
> Impact Postproduction
> 35 Green Street
> Edinburgh EH1 7TF
>
> 1 March 1999
>
> Dear Mrs Smith
>
> **Postproduction assistant position**
>
> I am currently studying languages at the University of Cambridge and will be graduating in June. I write to enquire whether there are any postproducer assistant, or similar, vacancies within your company.
>
> As you can see from my Curriculum Vitae, I already have a considerable amount of experience in this field, working through my penultimate year at university for Special Effects Limited. I have also gained valuable production experience working for Cambridge Student Television.
>
> I have been particularly keen to work for your company since seeing examples of your work, including the latest James Bond title sequence.
>
> If there are any suitable vacancies, I would welcome the opportunity to meet you.
>
> Yours sincerely
>
>
> Joanne Green
>
> 55 Mollington Road
> Cambridge
> CB5 6TG
>
> Tel. 01223 123456
> Joanne@madeup.net
>
> Enclosure: Curriculum Vitae

Figure 11.1 Sample `on spec' letter

To Conclude

Applying for jobs on spec can pay wonderful dividends. Not only do you have a chance to land a job you really want, you could very possibly have done it without being in competition with anyone else at all!

However, one word of warning. Don't make it your only method of job-hunting. You need to combine it with as many other methods as you possibly can for optimum results!

And if your first attempt doesn't go quite as you planned – don't give up. Every time you make a telephone call or write a letter you gain experience. With experience comes confidence. It would be misleading to suggest that the very first time you picked the phone up an employer said, 'Fantastic, you're just what I've been looking for' (although it did happen to me once).

In common with every method of job-hunting, you need to accept that applying to lots of different organizations is the only way to assure yourself of the success you deserve.

12 How Applications Are Processed: The Reality

The Dream

Your letter and its accompanying CV, land on the director's desk. 'Hold all calls!' he yells at his assistant. 'Don't disturb me until lunch time. I've got something very important to read.'

Wouldn't that be brilliant? Unfortunately, the only place it ever will happen for most of us, is in our dreams.

The Reality

Your letter and its accompanying CV, land on the director's desk, together with 25 others. 'I haven't got time for this,' he grumbles to his assistant. 'Here, you find me a handful worth interviewing.'

This may sound a little disappointing. After all the work you put into preparing your CV and covering letter, it's not even going to be looked at by the decision maker. What's even worse, the amount of time that's going to be spent deciding whether your application is worthy of further consideration will probably be less than 30 seconds!

What Really Happens

When an employer is faced with a pile of letters, the ones which don't look presentable get put on the rejection pile immediately without ever being read (that's why the presentation of your CV and covering letter are covered in such detail in this book). Then, the letters which *do* look presentable, are scanned briefly. Any letter full of spelling mistakes, or which makes the reader feel the applicant is totally unsuitable for the job, is also rejected.

The remaining letters and their accompanying CVs or application forms, are read more carefully. The choice of who will be called to interview (or the next stage of the recruitment process) will be made from this final selection only.

Will They Read the Whole CV?

No, not very thoroughly at this stage. Assuming your application is well presented, the employer will be looking for evidence of your suitability for the job. Once they've found some evidence, your application will probably be given to someone else to fix up an interview.

What About the Stuff I Wrote About My Hobbies?

At this stage, it's unlikely anyone will pay much attention to your leisure interests. Having said that, if you haven't got any work experience, your hobbies might be the only thing (other than academic qualifications) that an employer can use to gauge your suitability. So it is very important to include them.

What you've written about your leisure interests will probably not be read until an interviewer tries to find out more about your personality. That's good, if it gives you a chance to demonstrate your finer points. It's bad, if you've put down ballroom dancing and don't know the difference between a fox trot and a waltz.

The Good News

Before you give up and go home, there is some good news. Very good news, actually. Employers don't like to make a big song and dance about this, but in general, most of the applications

they receive are very badly presented, appalling, in fact.
It is surprising how many people write messy letters, or whose letters are littered with misspellings and corrections, and are generally grubby.

The good news is that you don't have to be a million times better than everyone else to get on the 'interview' pile. First impressions are everything. Just 10 per cent better will get your application on to the 'reading' pile straight away, regardless of your experience.

Does the Same Apply to Application Forms?

Yes, it does. Even forms which are scanned electronically have to be well presented or the computer can't 'see' them. That means filling in all the boxes, being very tidy, keeping the paper clean, making sure the paper doesn't get creased up, using the correct colour pen and following all the directions carefully.

I Haven't Heard Anything – Now What?

It isn't difficult to find out how your application is progressing. If you've applied to a small company, a quick telephone call will give you an idea of what's going on. Be prepared to go straight into 'interview mode' if you get to speak to a decision maker. That person may even be in the process of sorting out the applications when you call. Your CV might be right in front of them and who can resist asking a few questions?

You can ask questions too. This will demonstrate your interest and your enthusiasm. Just ensure you ask questions that relate to the job, the organization or the timetable (eg, when they're planning to conduct the interviews). Ditch anything irrelevant, don't ask any 'what's in it for me' questions, and don't discuss the weather!

Tracking Your Application

Many organizations (and not just large ones) will be able to track your application via their computer system. Again, you will have to telephone to find out. As always when you're talking to prospective employers, remember to:

▪ smile;

▪ be friendly and polite to everyone;

▪ have the details of the job you applied for (and the research you've done on the organization) in front of you. It's easy to forget things when you're feeling under stress;

▪ keep the copy of your letter, your CV or application form close too, so you remember what you said.

Read more about tracking your application, and even more suggestions as to how to tip the scales in your favour, in Chapter 19.

13 Modern Recruitment Techniques

Recruitment is no longer an art, it's a science. If you want to land a job, you'll need to know about the latest recruitment techniques.

The trend is for you to be sent a letter inviting you to come along to the organization's premises (or an external test centre). The letter will say something like, 'There will be a number of tests, an interview and a presentation. Please arrive at 9.30 am and expect to allow three hours.'

If you get a letter like this, you'll know that you'll be up against something a little more involved than a straightforward one-to-one interview.

Why Are These Methods Used?

It's quite simple. Employers have woken up to the fact that recruiting the wrong people costs a great deal of money. For a start recruitment advertising is expensive; the per centimetre rate for 'Sits Vac' is usually far higher than any other type of advertising. Speaking to candidates on the telephone, sifting through applications, and interviewing all take up a great deal of time and someone has to be paid to do it.

Finally, taking someone on only to discover that they cannot do the job, and/or hate the job and leave, is not an option any longer. It is vitally important to get it right, first time. That's why more and more organizations are turning to so-called 'scientifically proven' methods to select their staff.

Who Uses Them?

You are more likely to come up against psychometric testing and other 'high tech' methods if you apply to a large organization. Small to medium sized enterprises (SMEs) still rely to a great extent on the traditional interview for their recruitment decisions, although this is changing.

Psychometric Tests

Verbal Reasoning

Despite the name, verbal reasoning papers are *written* tests, which are taken in exam-like conditions. Generally you will be expected to answer between 30 and 50 multiple choice questions in less than half an hour. You will be strictly timed. Putting you under pressure is intentional.

An employer might give you one of these tests to do by yourself, but you're more likely to find yourself in a hall with 99 other people all taking it as well.

Verbal reasoning tests are used to determine your ability to read and understand words, but that's not all. Also on trial is your:

- understanding of what you've read;

- ability to pick out the salient points from the information given;

- ability to relate or present these points to other people.

Figure 13.1 shows some example verbal reasoning questions (answers at the end of the chapter).

Test 1

WORD POWER
Choose the word that best completes the following sentences.

1 Adept means the same as:

A	B	C	D	E
energetic	inefficient	enthusiastic	awkward	skilful

2 Hard is to soft as hot is to:

A	B	C	D	E
cool	warm	cold	icy	tepid

3 A straight edge should be used to ensure that the ends of the shelves are correctly:

A	B	C	D	E
tightened	aligned	concentric	separated	flat

4 Which of the following words is closest in meaning to vertical?

A	B	C	D	E
horizontal	parallel	straight	perpendicular	flat

Figure 13.1 Examples of verbal reasoning questions © SHL Group plc 1998

Handy Hints on Verbal Reasoning Papers

- Verbal reasoning papers are marked very quickly, often by placing a specially designed grid over the paper. This means you have to be careful about marking your answers clearly. Make sure you follow any instructions for correcting wrong answers or you will lose marks.

- Help yourself assimilate written information by reading books and newspapers regularly. Crossword puzzles are useful for practising verbal critical reasoning.

- Your careers service should be able to give you some practice papers. Other sources of practice material are listed in Further Reading at the back of the book.

- Keeping up-to-date with current affairs is also a good idea since there could be questions relating to items in the news or the general economic situation.

- Verbal reasoning tests come in varying levels of difficulty. The higher the level of job you are applying for, the harder the questions.

- Before the test begins, if there is anything you don't understand, ask.

- You will have very little time to answer each question. Try not to panic. Work through the questions one by one, if you come up against one you simply cannot answer leave it until the end. Go back to it if you have time.

- If you finish all the questions before the end of the test, go back and re-check your answers. Never sit and stare into space!

- Don't worry too much if you failed to complete the test or if you think you got some of the answers wrong. Most people taking the test will be feeling this way. You won't need

Modern Recruitment Techniques

to have scored top marks to continue further into the assessment process.

- If you really think you messed up, say so. Give a good reason and be honest and you could be offered the opportunity to retake.

Numerical Reasoning

Numerical reasoning papers are similar to verbal reasoning papers in that they are written tests, which are taken in exam-like conditions. You will be strictly timed. Putting you under pressure is intentional.

Again, you might be given one of these tests to do by yourself, but you're more likely to find yourself in a hall with 99 other people all taking it at the same time.

Numerical reasoning tests are used to determine your ability to think with, and analyse numbers. If you are going for a job in which there is any element of figure work, be prepared to take one of these tests.

Sometimes you will find the questions are all the same type, ie all number sequences. But number problems can be presented in a variety of ways. There could be:

- graphs;
- sequences;
- pie charts;
- plain figure work.

Figure 13.2 shows some example numerical reasoning questions (answers at the end of the chapter).

Landing Your First Job

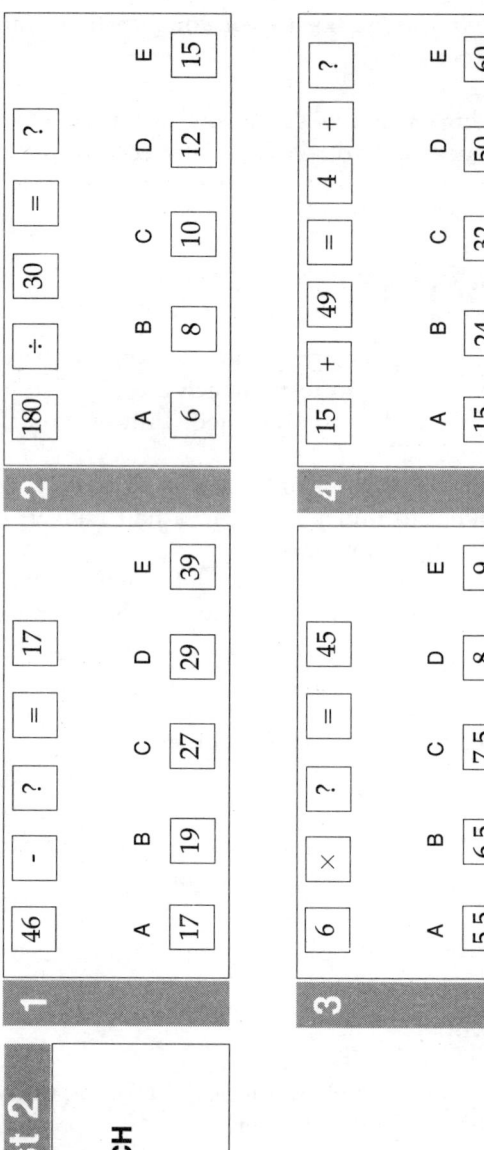

Figure 13.2 Examples of numerical reasoning questions © SHL Group plc 1998

Handy Hints on Numerical Reasoning Papers

- Numerical reasoning papers are marked very quickly, often by placing a specially designed grid over the paper. This means you have to be careful about marking your answers clearly. Make sure you follow any instructions for correcting wrong answers or you will lose marks.

- Number puzzles are useful for practising numerical reasoning. Going over your times tables will also help.

- Your careers service should be able to give you some practice papers. Other sources of practice material are listed in Further Reading at the back of the book.

- Sometimes calculators are allowed. Take one just in case.

- Before the test begins, if there is anything you don't understand, ask.

- You will have very little time to answer each question. Try not to panic. Work through the questions one by one and if you come up against one you simply cannot answer, leave it until the end. Go back to it if you have time.

- If you finish all the questions before the end of the test, go back and re-check your answers. Use the time productively.

- Don't worry too much if you failed to complete the test, or if you think you got some of the answers wrong. Most people taking the test will be feeling this way. You won't need to have scored top marks to continue further along the assessment process.

- As with verbal reasoning papers, you will often be given an opportunity to talk to someone after the test is over. It might be a sort of 'mini interview' where you are asked how you felt about the test and how you thought you did.

If you think you messed it up, say so. Say, 'I think I messed it up because...' Give a good reason.

Personality Questionnaires

Personality questionnaires are also written exam papers, and are very popular with employers. They often have a great many questions, sometimes as many as 250. They are all about you – how you see yourself and how you think other people see you. Sometimes you are required to give a 'yes' or 'no' answer. Sometimes you have to rate (on a scale of one to five) your agreement or disagreement with a given statement, for instance 'I like to be the leader'.

Personality questionnaires are used to test your:

- motivation and thinking style;

- emotional responses to given situations;

- how you get on with other people;

- occupational preferences, eg whether you are a good match for the job on offer;

- your honesty – these are growing in popularity.

Figure 13.3 shows two different examples of personality questionnaires.

Handy Hints on Personality Questionnaires

There are no 'right' or 'wrong' answers.

- Generally, an employer would not reject anyone on the basis of this type of test. Your completed paper is more likely to be used by an interviewer looking for inspiration. For instance, if you answered a question asking if you stay calm under pressure with a 'yes', your interviewer might ask you to talk about a situation when you did just that.

- Be honest. Don't answer in the way you think you *should*. These tests have built in safeguards which, although undetectable to the untrained eye, will immediately alert the employer to the fact that you've tried to 'cheat'.

- Another reason why you should answer the questions honestly, is that it's the only way you'll be able to complete the test. If you spend time thinking, 'What would be the best answer here?' you'll waste time and end up not finishing.

Other Psychometric Tests

Verbal reasoning, numerical reasoning and personality tests are not the only psychometric tests available, although for the most part they are the most commonly used. Also available are tests that measure logic, accuracy, technical ability, perceptual ability, spatial ability and so on. Describing them all would fill the rest of this book.

If you think you might come up against one of these tests, ask your careers service to provide you with practice papers. Alternatively, see Further Reading at the back of the book for suggestions.

1 Rating Statements

In this example you are asked to rate yourself on a number of phrases or statements. After reading each statement mark your answer according to the following rules:

Fill in circle 1   If you strongly disagree with the statement

Fill in circle 2   If you disagree with the statement

Fill in circle 3   If you are unsure

Fill in circle 4   If you agree with the statement

Fill in circle 5   If you strongly agree with the statement

The first statement has already been completed for you. The person has agreed that 'I enjoy meeting new people' is an accurate description of him/herself.

Now try questions 2 to 6 for yourself by completely filling in the circle that is most true for you

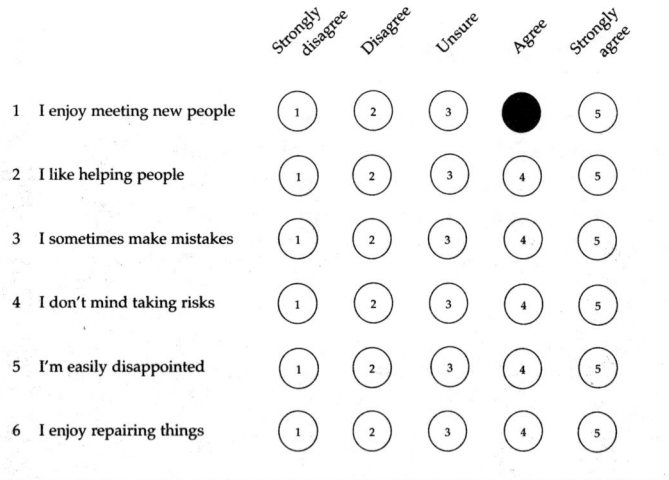

Figure 13.3 Examples of personality questionnaires
© SHL Group plc 1998

2 Making Choices

In this example you are given a block of four statements: A, B, C and D. Your task is to choose the statement which you think is most true or typical of you in your everyday behaviour and then choose the one which is least true or typical of you. Indicate your choices by filling in the appropriate circle in the row marked 'M' (for Most) and in the next row 'L' (for Least).

The first block has been completed for you. The person has chosen, 'Enjoys organizing people' as most true (or typical) and 'Seeks variety' as being least true (or typical) of him/herself. Now try questions 2, 3 and 4 yourself.

I am the sort of person who...

1   A   Has a wide circle of friends
    B   Enjoys organizing people
    C   Relaxes easily
    D   Seeks variety

2   A   Helps people with their problems
    B   Develops new approaches
    C   Has lots of energy
    D   Enjoys social activities

3   A   Has lots of new ideas
    B   Feels calm
    C   Likes to understand things
    D   Is easy to get on with

4   A   Enjoys organizing events
    B   Sometimes gets angry
    C   Is talkative
    D   Resolves conflicts at work

Landing Your First Job

In Tray Exercises

You are likely to come up against 'in tray' exercises when you apply for any sort of management or trainee management position.
In tray exercises are used to find out how well you:

- prioritize;
- evaluate;
- make decisions;
- react under pressure;
- work accurately.

All are essential management skills. What happens is that you are given around one hour to prioritize say, 20 tasks. In other words, you have to decide which task you would tackle first, which one you would tackle next and so on, until you have the entire list in the right order, from 1 to 20.
You then have to explain your reasons for doing so by writing one or two sentences for one on a separate piece of paper or a chart. Here is an example 'in tray' question:

> Imagine you are a trainee buyer in our organization. You've been on holiday for two weeks and today is your first day back at work. It is 9 am. You have a meeting with your manager at 11 am and there are 20 items of correspondence in your 'in tray' all requiring your immediate attention. Put the 20 items in priority order, and explain your reasons.

How to Tackle an In Tray Exercise

So you have to put all the items in the correct order – but what is the correct order? The first thing to realize is that there isn't a 'right' or a 'wrong' order at all. It's all a matter of interpretation.

Look at the list of items, and you will notice:

- some of them will look complicated, some will obviously be very simple;

- some will look as if they may take several hours to complete, others could probably be done in minutes;

- some tasks will look boring, others will sound quite enjoyable;

- some items are nothing to do with the actual business at all.

It's very tempting to say you would do the easiest, the quickest, or the most enjoyable ones first, but the real trick is to decide which are the most important. These must go at the top of your list.

By giving you an 'in tray' exercise to do, the organization is looking to see if *your* idea of what is important, is the same as *theirs*. They want to see if you can decide what's essential and what isn't. In other words, they want to know whether you are capable of making good business decisions.

Here are some of the factors you need to take into account when you make that decision.

- Which tasks are essential to the business, which ones will have less of an effect if you don't get on with them right away?

- What about the date on individual items? Remember, you're supposed to have been on holiday for two weeks. Some of the oldest items may be more urgent than those which are only a few days old.

- Who does the item in your imaginary 'in tray' come from? You might want to give something from the Chief Executive a greater priority than one from a member of your imaginary staff.

Finally, remember to explain yourself. The employer will want to know why you made the decisions you did.

Group Exercises

Group exercises involve more than one candidate. Generally, you will be expected to carry out a task, or sit round a table and take part in a discussion, with four or five other candidates.

Also in the room will be two or three assessors. Their job is to observe and assess. They will sit unobtrusively behind you or in the corner, and they will take notes. The only time they will speak is to explain what they want you to do, and to tell you that time's up. Some organizations will allocate one assessor to each candidate so there could be six of you and six of *them* in the room at the same time!

Here is an example of the sort of exercise you might be given:

> You (all the candidates) are a lottery committee. Each of you represents the interests of a different 'good cause'. Your task is to decide how you would allocate the money; which 'good cause' would benefit the most, which would receive the next largest amount, and so on until you've come up with a priority list.
>
> The list of good causes (one for each candidate) could be:

- a minibus for a hospital;
- equipment for a children's playground;
- wheelchair ramps in an old people's home;
- a holiday for a group of disabled youngsters.

How to do the Exercise

First of all you will need to take part in the discussion. It's no good sitting there and saying nothing. You need to think of reasons why your good cause should get the money and ague convincingly. However, you will not be marked on whether your case wins or not. This is what you *will* be marked on:

- how well you work with other people in this group situation;

- whether you take other people's views into consideration;

- whether you are willing to compromise;

- how persuasively you can argue your own case (or another person's case);

- what role you take on in the group as a whole.

The idea is for the group to come up with a priority list *by consensus*. You do have to put your case as convincingly as you can, but steamrollering everyone will do nothing but irritate.

Another thing to remember is that each candidate has been given a different good cause. Some of them will be more worthy than others. This is quite deliberate. If you have been given a weak brief, the assessors will be interested in whether you recognize that fact. They'll want to know whether you are willing to concede that another person's case is better than yours, and even whether you are willing to argue on their behalf.

What Role to Play

The role you take in the group will be watched by the assessors. Sometimes they'll appoint one candidate to act as group leader. If you are allocated the role, then your job is to keep the discussion going, encourage all the candidates to contribute, and make sure everyone is aware of the time deadline. You'll also be expected to bring the discussion to a conclusion at the end of the allotted time.

If no leader is appointed, don't worry if it isn't your natural inclination to assume the role of chairperson. It's difficult to be something you're not. Just involve yourself in the exercise as much as you can and try to forget about being watched.

If you get a chance to talk with one of the assessors after the exercise is finished, be as honest as you can about yourself when they ask, 'How do you think you did in that exercise?'

Group Exercises That Require Technical Know-how

Here's an example of another group exercise; and it's the sort of thing you might come up against where you're going for a job requiring a certain level of technical knowledge:

> You and five other candidates are given a mountain of Lego bricks and are asked to build a bridge. The design of the bridge, ie its height, length and width (or whatever you're supposed to be building) is usually specified.

It doesn't take a genius to work out that, apart from technical competence, your ability to work with other people, your planning skills, analytical thinking, ability to communicate ideas and willingness to listen to others, are also being assessed.

So remember to:

- voice your ideas – don't keep them to yourself;

- listen to other people and don't rubbish their ideas – give them a go instead;

- be involved in the problem – don't stay on the sidelines;

- try and enjoy it, and be yourself. If you do you'll be much less likely to feel intimidated by the observers.

Problem-solving Exercises

Problem-solving exercises are another type of group exercise. They involve the same set up as described above, only this time the group has to find the answer to a problem or a puzzle.

Each person is given a different snippet of information, usually written on a card or a piece of paper. Each bit of information is meaningless by itself: the problem can only be solved by everybody working together, sharing their information and helping one another.

The problem always has one solution. You will probably find that, apart from coming up with the right answer, you are asked (as a group) to explain *why* it is the right answer. You will be told you have a certain amount of time to solve the problem and that you will be strictly timed. Putting you under pressure is intentional.

How to do the Exercise

The assessors will be hoping that your group is able to solve the puzzle, but that isn't the only thing they're looking for, and it isn't the most important either. What they're marking is:

- whether you are able to pull out the relevant facts from the information you've been given – some of it will be red herrings;

- whether you can think creatively;

- how well you work in a team and whether you co-operate with others;

- whether you are willing to give other people's ideas a go;

- whether you help other people.

You can see that by watching you and how you behave in this situation, the organization can get a pretty good idea of the sort of person you are. They can see you interacting with others, cooperating, helping and encouraging others (or not). They can see if you get involved, or sit on the sidelines and let others do the work.

Remember to:

- listen to other people;

- avoid criticizing other people's ideas. Give them a go instead;

- be involved in the problem. Try and enjoy it, and be yourself. If you do you'll be much less likely to feel intimidated by the observers.

Presentations

A presentation is where you stand up and talk to an audience. Usually a presentation lasts five or 10 minutes, but it could be longer.

Being asked to give a presentation is very common. You can expect to be hit with this one for all sorts of different jobs. You are *most* likely to be asked to give a presentation if you are applying for a trainee management position, or a job in sales.

What Subject Will I Have to Talk About?

If you're lucky, *you* might be allowed to choose your own subject. If so, make it interesting because sending the audience off to sleep won't be smiled upon.

If the organization picks the subject, it could be anything from one of the hobbies you mentioned on your CV, to a current news item. You could be asked to talk about yourself and what you would bring to the job, or an issue relating in some way to the organization's business.

Topics which relate to the organization's business (and the job you've applied for) are very common, and often require a lot of research. Here is an example:

You are invited to attend an interview in a week's time. The job is trainee buyer with a multinational food retailer. As part of your assessment, you've been asked to give a ten-minute presentation on, 'How I would research the ice cream market to find a new 'best-selling' flavour.'

It is clear that they are expecting you to research the subject, in this case, ice cream. This is what to do.

- Don't panic. You have a whole week to prepare.

   – Ring up and ask for more information if they haven't sent you anything.
   – Who will your presentation be given to? How many people? Will other candidates be there?

- Start researching.

   – What ice cream flavours do they currently sell? Go along to one of their shops and find out.
   – What are the current best-selling flavours? Speak to the manager of that department and ask. Do people buy exotic new flavours, or do they stick to ones they're familiar with?
   – What's the competition doing? Visit other supermarkets and newsagents to see what's available.
   – Telephone the head office and ask for the department that deals with ice cream. Ask them to send you information on the product, if they haven't already done so. Ask how *they* go about researching the market. How do they decide which new flavours to sell? Tell them why you want to know and you're bound to find somebody sympathetic enough to help.

- Gather the information together.

   – Make a complete list of points; write down all your ideas.
   – Arrange the points into groups.
   – Decide which groups will form your introduction, the main argument and the conclusion.

- Try and avoid using jargon. Keep it simple.
- Make sure you have a beginning, a middle and an end, plus a title.
- Are there any audio or visual aids you can use. Any pictures, or lists of flavours you can hand round?

■ Try your presentation out.

- Stand up and give a practice presentation to your friends or family.
- Ask them to time you, to make sure you don't go over the allotted time.
- Ask for feedback. What did they think of it? What did they like? Which bits didn't they understand?
- Alternatively, use a tape recorder (or a mirror) and try it out on yourself.

■ On the day, remember to:

- take your notes and any audio/visual aids with you;
- try and relax. Remember all the other candidates will be going through the same thing, and most of them will have done less preparation than you;
- Dress smartly. If you feel confident it will show.

■ During the presentation:

- smile, look at your audience and try and make eye contact;
- introduce yourself and the title of your presentation;
- don't speak too quickly;
- don't make any racist or sexist comments;
- aim for your voice to reach the back of the room, so everyone can hear you;
- be enthusiastic. Sound like you're really interested in the subject;
- don't worry if you make a mistake. Make a joke out of it instead. 'I didn't mean that, actually. Just the opposite in fact'.

Before you begin, say, 'Can everyone hear me okay?' If you can't be heard, your audience will fall asleep.

Whatever you do, don't stop in the middle and give up. Tell yourself 'the show must go on' and keep going. The fact that you've researched your subject and practised the presentation should give you a lot of confidence.

Being Expected to Give a Presentation With Little or no Notice

Here are a few tips on giving a presentation at short notice.

- Don't panic. Remember, the other candidates will also be unprepared.

- Use any time you do have efficiently. Don't think, 'I'll worry about it tomorrow.'

- Don't be caught out. Being asked to give a presentation at short notice is very common so have a possible topic ready (keep the notes in your briefcase).

- Whatever you talk about, be enthusiastic.

- Don't worry about other candidates sitting in on your presentation; you'll get to watch them too.

Coping With the Competition

One of the worst things about having to give a presentation is seeing all the other candidates sitting there in the audience, willing you to dry up or burst into tears.

In fairness, the majority of companies who use presentations as part of their recruitment process are not pitting you against those other candidates at all. What you are in competition with is a general standard. This means that if you *all* perform well, you'll *all* be in with a chance.

So when it's someone else's turn to get up and talk, give them the support they deserve.

Using Audio-visual Aids

Some examples of audio-visual aids are overhead projectors and flip-charts. It's well known that we remember more information that we see *and* hear, than information we just hear. Therefore, you'd be forgiven for thinking that using an audio-visual aid could only *improve* your presentation.

This is not necessarily true! If you are offered the use of one, think carefully. There are pitfalls, as well as advantages to using them.

Overhead Projectors

The use of an overhead projector can give your presentation a very professional feel, if – and it's a big if – you know how to use them. With enough time, and good graphics software, you can prepare all sorts of pretty pictures to impress your audience. Graphs, pie charts, diagrams, pictures: anything you want, you name it.

Without computer graphics, or the time to prepare them all, hand writing on the acetate is the next best thing. This is okay for a rough and ready presentation, but won't give the same polished, professional feel.

Here are a few tips for using an overhead projector in your presentation.

- Stick to plain text, the fancy stuff is difficult to read from a distance.

- Don't use too much text at one time.

- Be as original as possible. Avoid using too much clip art; your audience will have seen it all before.

- Make sure you place the acetate onto the projector the right way up, or your pictures will appear upside down! Imagine you are facing the audience, with the screen behind you. Place the acetate down so that you can read it.

- Before you get started, check that everyone can see the screen.

- Once you have started, don't stand in front of the screen.

- Talk to the audience, not the screen!

The biggest pitfall with using overhead projectors is bad luck. The classic case is spending a whole week preparing your presentation only to have the projector blow up when you switch it on!

Flip-charts

One advantage to using a flip-chart is that you don't have to worry about technology. It's quick and simple. All you do is write on the paper with a thick felt-tip pen.

Tips For Using a Flip-chart in Your Presentation

- Before you start talking, check that everyone in the room can see it.

- Once you have started talking, don't stand in front of it. Stand to one side.

- Don't hide behind it either – you'll look even more nervous than you really are.

- Talk to the audience, not the flip-chart.

- Don't lean on the flip-chart or it will definitely fall over!

- If you move around during your presentation, give the flip-chart a wide berth. It's easier than you think to trip over the legs.

- Make sure your writing is large enough to be seen.

- Use two or three colours to make it look a bit more interesting, but don't go completely over the top.

- If you write while you're speaking, try and write in a straight line and not at an angle.

If you have to speak for, say, 10 minutes, you're probably going to cover three or four different areas of the topic in question. A simple and effective way of using a flip-chart is to write these three or four different points on the paper, and have it sitting there throughout your speech. Use bullet points; just a few words will suffice. You don't need to use complete sentences. You can refer to it, 'My second point is...'

The beauty of this method is that your audience sees the structure of your presentation right up there in front of them. They know what you're going to talk about during your introduction, the middle, and how you're going to summarize at the end. They'll also know how much longer they've got to sit there and listen!

Work Experience

It's always possible that you'll be invited to spend a day doing the job you've applied for. This can be a daunting prospect. The thought of spending a whole day being assessed by your new boss *before* you've been offered the job would be difficult for anyone, but there are advantages.

Although you'll have to dress smartly, and be on your best 'interview mode' behaviour all day, think of the experience as a wonderful opportunity to find out what your boss, your new work mates, and the job itself are really like.

Although the dos and don'ts are really the same for any interview situation, also remember to:

- arrive on time;
- be enthusiastic;
- take an interest in your new colleagues;
- don't indulge in any gossiping behind the boss's back;
- thank them for the opportunity of working with them;
- give them feedback.

Giving feedback is absolutely vital if you want the job. If they made you feel welcome, if you enjoyed yourself, if you still want to work there, make sure you tell them.

Future Developments

Video-conferencing

Already established in the insurance and medical industries, the use of video-conferencing is now extending into recruitment. This method is currently favoured by large organizations with branches in different locations. Think how convenient it is for them (and you too) if they interview locally instead of making candidates travel hundreds of miles, or even overseas.

Being interviewed in front of a computer with a camera pointing at your face can't be the easiest thing to do, but at least your interviewer won't know you're wearing a grass skirt! (They will if a video-conferencing 'room system' is used.)

Joking aside, if you know you're going to be interviewed in this way, still dress as if you were going along to a face-to-face interview: smartly. And that means right down to your shoes! Also, just a few extra tips:

- wear bright, plain colours, but not too much white;
- avoid patterns and stripes like the plague;
- look at the camera, not your feet;
- smile a lot.

Computerized Assessments and Multimedia

The up and coming technique, the idea is that you sit at a computer and watch a video of a situation (usually a work scenario). When the video ends, you stay seated at the computer and plough through a load of questions.

Stress Indicators

At present, this method is fairly undeveloped, but it wouldn't be surprising if tests to measure how you cope with stress start appearing soon. However, if you can cope with the tests described in this chapter, especially the group exercises and presentations, then believe me, you can cope with anything!

Answers to Test Questions

Figure 13.1: Verbal reasoning: 1E, 2C, 3B, 4D
Figure 13.2: Numerical reasoning: 1D, 2A, 3C, 4E

14 Preparing For Your Interview

You have been offered an interview, but how should you prepare? What can you do to give yourself the best chance of landing the job?

Well first of all, you can afford to be confident. Be assured, once you've got to this stage, you are already on the short-list. Only the most promising candidates are invited to meet their prospective employer, and you are one of them. But you still need to prepare. To start with, you will need information.

What Sort of Interview Will it Be?

The organization you applied to may write to you, but they're just as likely to telephone and ask you when you would like to come in. During the conversation, see if you can find out a little more about the interview itself. Will it be a:

- one-to-one interview, where you are interviewed by just one person. If so, who will it be – your prospective boss or someone from the personnel department?

- two-to-one interview, where there will be two interviewers present. One of them may be your possible new boss, the other is likely to be *their* boss. Be prepared for only one of them to do most of the talking.

- panel interview, where you will be interviewed by three or more people. This is the norm for jobs in hospitals, local authorities and local government. The intention is not to intimidate you, but rather to save you being interviewed by each and every department that needs to okay recruitment decisions. Watch out for panel interviews where the ultimate decision maker sits quietly in the corner simply watching the proceedings. Try and maintain eye contact with everyone.

- group interview, where you will be assessed alongside other candidates. Generally, you may be given exercises to do with the other candidates (covered in Chapter 13) but normally, actual 'interviews' are not shared.

The more you can discover at this stage, the more prepared you will be. Also, make sure you've got the basics right. Do you know:

- Where you have to go for your interview. Write the address down while you're on the telephone. If you're going by car, ask, 'Is there anywhere I can park?' If you're travelling by train, find out which is the nearest station.

- When is the interview. Write down the time and date. Don't be shy about asking for an alternative if the time they suggest isn't convenient.

- Whether they want you to bring anything with you, such as examples of your work.

All very basic things, but all vitally important. Imagine how embarrassing it would be to turn up at the wrong location, on the wrong day.

Handling the Call

This telephone call (to sort out the time and place of the interview) is actually part of the recruitment process itself. Your chances of landing the job can be enhanced or ruined, depending on how you handle the call.

Preparing For Your Interview

The person who you speak to might be the receptionist or secretary, or they may be your actual interviewer. Either way, aim for them to think, 'They sound nice, I'm looking forward to meeting this person', rather than, 'They were rude, they won't fit in here.'

Researching

Although this subject has already been covered in Chapter 5, I think it is important to say a little more about it here. If you can demonstrate some knowledge of the organization during your interview you will have gained a very great advantage over all the other candidates. The reasons are simple:

- The organization will be looking to employ someone who wants to work specifically for *them* (as opposed to any other organization). Demonstrating an interest will show them you are serious about your choice of employer.

- It's quite possible you will be asked, 'Why do you want to work for us?' during the interview. If you don't know what the organization does, you won't be able to answer the question.

- Your interviewer will be flattered that you have taken an interest in them. Interviewers are just people. They want to be noticed!

- Hardly anyone else will do it.

So make the effort to find out what product or service the organization offers. There's nothing to stop you ringing and asking for a brochure, looking at their advertising, visiting their Web site. Getting information isn't just for the purpose of helping you to make a good impression during your interview. You need information to be able to decide whether you really want to work for them, and what questions you want to ask when you get to the interview.

How to Dress

It goes without saying that your clothes should be clean, tidy and presentable, but what should you actually wear? Well, for the most part, your interviewer will be dressed quite smartly, most likely in a suit. If you turn up wearing jeans, you'll probably feel underdressed and out of place.

The same goes for high fashion, or anything else over the top. Unless you are applying for a job in the fashion industry, employers are usually on the conservative side, so multicoloured hair and green lipstick is out. This is especially important where you are applying for a position involving contact with customers. Here, the ability to look presentable will be part of the job specification. Turn up wearing something completely unsuitable and you'll have blown your chances as soon as you walk through the door.

If you are female, going along in the shortest skirt you possess may not be a good idea. The truth is, if you dress very provocatively, a *female* interviewer may take an instant dislike to you. You are running the risk of being seen as a threat, and that's unlikely to land you the job. Even if you are absolutely certain that your interviewer is male, you're bound to be seen by at least one female member of staff. One word, or even a look, is all it takes for your chances to be ruined. The same goes for lots of jewellery and too much perfume. Of course, a little bit of perfume will probably give you confidence – just don't go along smelling like you've poured the whole bottle over your head!

Wear a dress (or skirt) with a jacket over the top, or a suit, and choose materials that don't crease too much. As far as your shoes are concerned; stick to smart and comfortable. Stiletto heels are unsuitable, and open-toed sandals and flip-flops are too casual, even in the middle of a heatwave. Imagine you're already working for the organization; now choose something that you would wear on an important day, for instance, if a valued customer were coming into the office to see you. Even if you are after a job where you'll *never* have to wear a suit, looking smart always creates a good impression.

If you are male, aim to look businesslike. For instance, a white or blue shirt will make a better impression than a fluorescent

Preparing For Your Interview

green one. An unobtrusive tie is preferable. Again, it is safest to imagine you're already working for the organization and to choose something that you would wear on an important day. Even if you are after a job where you'll *never* have to wear a suit, looking smart still creates a good impression. Make sure your shoes are polished.

The best advice for both men and women is to wear something you feel comfortable and confident in, and go as yourself. If you're still unsure, ring the organization and speak to the receptionist who will be happy to tell you if there is any sort of 'dress code' in operation.

Finally, this may sound obvious, but make sure your nails are clean. There's nothing more off-putting than having to shake hands with someone who looks like they haven't washed their hands properly.

> **Tip:** Some organizations make a point of peeping inside your car while you're being interviewed. Yes it's true! If you plan to park your car in the company car park, make sure it's clean, both inside and out.

What to Take With You

What sort of interview is it going to be? What sort of job are you going for? If you are an illustrator going for a job at a design studio, obviously you'll have to bring your portfolio along with you. If there is any evidence you can produce to demonstrate your competence, bring it along.

This doesn't extend to examination certificates or references. For a start, your exam results should already be detailed on your CV and it's most unlikely that you will ever be asked to produce the actual documents. Handing over written references can make you appear desperate, and anyway, most employers prefer to obtain references for themselves.

Bringing a newspaper or a book to read while you're waiting to be interviewed isn't a good idea either. Far better to get hold of a copy of the company brochure if they have one. After all, your interviewer will be looking for someone who shows an interest in their organization. Seeing you with a copy of their brochure can only impress.

If you do take the company brochure along, make sure you've read it. Your interviewer is bound to start the interview off by asking what you know about their organization. If you can demonstrate that you've taken the time to find out a little about what they do, your interview will be off to a flying start. Remember, very few people take the trouble to find out anything about the organization they are applying to. If you do, you'll have an immediate advantage.

Other things to take with you include:

- several copies of your CV. Make sure you take the same version as the one you sent, and make sure you know what it says;

- a notebook for writing things down during the interview.

- examples of your work if this would be useful;

- your glasses if you need them. There's always a chance that you may be presented with a questionnaire or an application form. If this happens, you'll need to be able to see what you're doing;

- a good pen to fill the forms in, and to take notes;

- a smart brief case or document case. If you don't possess one, borrow. Never use a scruffy old plastic bag.

Regarding the last point, many women wonder whether they should carry a briefcase *and* a handbag. There can't be anything more embarrassing than opening your briefcase during an interview, and having all your personal possessions fall out! So, if you're used to carrying a handbag, take one. Just make sure it looks presentable and isn't scruffy or dirty, and avoid beach bags and plastic bags.

Planning the Journey

Do you know exactly where the interview is? Which is the nearest station, or where to park the car? Do you need to get hold of a map of the area? If you're not sure, ring and ask. Don't leave anything to chance. Have a note of the interviewer's name and the organization's telephone number just in case you are unavoidably delayed and need to let them know you'll be late.

Chickening Out

This may seem like an obvious point, but once you've made the effort to get all the way there, don't chicken out and go home again! It isn't unusual for candidates to simply not turn up don't be one of them. Nothing terrible is going to happen to you during the interview. There is someone waiting for you, someone who wants to talk to you. That someone is really, really hoping that you will be the right person for the job. It would make their life so much easier if you were. So go for it.

Punctuality – Being Late

There's no doubt about it, arriving late creates a very bad impression. The interviewer will think, 'If she's late for the interview, she'll never get to work on time.' So allow plenty of time to get where you're going, and even extra time for minor hold-ups and traffic jams, etc. If anything can happen to slow you down, it will. The last thing you want is to arrive feeling completely stressed out.

If something happens that simply couldn't be foreseen, ring up and explain what's happened and give an expected time of arrival. Is this acceptable to your interviewer? Would they mind re-scheduling your appointment for a later one? If your reason is a genuine one, most employers will agree to re-schedule. Ringing up and explaining is much better than turning up late, or even worse, giving up and going home.

Aim to arrive just a little before the interview is scheduled to begin. This will give you enough time to have a quick look round, go to the bathroom if you need to, and do a bit of deep breathing to make you feel more relaxed.

Punctuality – Arriving Too Early

Arriving five minutes early isn't much of a problem, but any more than that is almost as bad as arriving late. Walking in half an hour early might be viewed by your prospective employer as being disrespectful. The hidden message you are giving out is, 'Here I am, you may see me now.' You're not taking any account of the fact that they will almost certainly be busy and not wish to be interrupted.

You might be quite happy to sit and wait, but *they* might feel you are expecting them to drop everything and see you immediately. And that doesn't create a very good impression.

So what should you do? You can always have a browse around the local shops or buy yourself a cup of coffee round the corner while you're waiting. But the most professional and impressive thing to do is to telephone them. Speak to the person who is going to interview you and explain that the journey was much quicker than expected. Then you can say something like, 'I can amuse myself without any problem until 10 o'clock (or whenever the interview was scheduled for) but if you would rather see me early, I'd be very happy to come in straight away.'

This way the message you are giving is, 'I know you're busy and I respect your time.' It is the professional approach, straightforward and respectful, without being in the least apologetic.

15 The Interview Begins

Arriving

Assuming you've allowed plenty of time to get to the interview, you will probably be feeling nervous, but not unduly rushed. If you're driving to the interview, make sure you park legally. There's nothing worse than being interrupted in the middle of an interview by somebody rushing in and shouting, 'Is that your car being towed away?' Joking aside, you don't want to be distracted by whether or not the meter has run out yet. And if you use the company car park, make sure you don't use a reserved spot.

As for your actual entrance; walk in, tell them your name and that you have an appointment at X o'clock with XYZ. Be friendly, and smile.

How to Treat People Other Than Your Interviewer

The only answer to this question is with courtesy and friendliness. That includes the receptionist, every member of staff at the company including the person who brings you a cup of tea while you're waiting to be interviewed, other candidates (if you meet them), and even that grumpy man in the car park. You never know; he could be your new boss. More about this subject in Chapter 18.

Of course, this friendly attitude has to extend to every single contact you have with the organization, not just when you come along for your interview. From the very first telephone call asking for an application form, to the call arranging the time and place of the interview, you must always, always be on your best behaviour. Be assured, one cross or sarcastic word spoken to even the most junior member of staff, will be reported straight back to the person whose job it is to decide whether to employ you or not.

While You're Waiting

As I've already said, it's better to be seen reading a company brochure than a detective novel! But you may not get a chance. As soon as you arrive, you may be asked to fill in a questionnaire, complete an official application or even take a test – and that's before you've even met the interviewer!

If you're asked to complete some sort of form then take as much care with it as possible. It's likely to be handed straight to the interviewer. They won't be very impressed if it has been filled out messily or is full of spelling mistakes. Use a reliable pen, black or blue ink is best. Never use a pencil, felt tip or coloured pencil because you'll look childish.

The main thing is not to be surprised. If you're prepared for a questionnaire or some sort of test as soon as you arrive (or even half way through the interview) it won't come as a shock.

Changes in Schedule

Sometimes you can be kept waiting. This is very irritating, and it won't do anything for your confidence, but try and stay calm. Whatever you do, don't get angry with the receptionist. Try and find out what is going on, and how long you can expect to wait. Your interviewer might be running late with his or her appointments, or something important may have come up that just can't wait.

The Introduction

Your interviewer comes to greet you, or you are shown into their office. Smile and shake hands. Try and make a conscious effort to

The Interview Begins

think, 'It's nice to meet you,' and your body language will say the same. You can even say it. You want them to like you straight away, and first impressions are extremely important. (Read more about handshakes later on in this chapter.)

At the same time as you shake hands, introduce yourself, and tell them your name. 'Alex Jones, nice to meet you.' Not all interviewers are well prepared. It's quite possible that they may have forgotten who they are seeing next, or they may have even lost your CV.

If there is more than one person in the room, say hello to them too. Shake *their* hand. Don't ignore anyone. By rights, the main interviewer should introduce you, but if not you'll have to do it yourself. And if you have no idea who they are, ask. You have a right to know who these people are and what they do. After all, one of them may be your new boss. Knowing who these people are makes it easier to understand where they're coming from when they start asking questions.

Where to Sit

Interviews in offices, especially one-to-one interviews, are usually conducted in a room with a desk. The interviewer will usually sit behind the desk and you will sit in front of it. Wait for your interviewer to offer you a seat before you sit down.

What happens if there is more than one chair in front of the desk? If the choice is between a chair facing the desk, and one sideways on, go for the chair that is sideways on. You will feel much more comfortable and relaxed there. Sitting sideways on to someone is less threatening and confrontational than sitting directly in front of them. It also creates the impression that you are more self-assured and confident, and that you want to 'get to know' your interviewer.

If there is no desk in between you and the interviewer, it may be a sign that they want to make the interview as informal and relaxed as possible.

And what happens if the chair you're supposed to take faces the window, and the sun is shining right in your eyes? There are two options. One is to say, 'Would you mind if I move the chair round to the side, the sun is shining right in my eyes?' and the other is to ask them to lower the blinds, if there are any. Being blinded by the light is not an option that any self-respecting person would accept.

And what if you have the misfortune to be interviewed by five people, all sitting behind a large imposing desk, and you're supposed to sit in a tiny little deckchair right in the middle of the room. There's not a lot you can do, except sit tall and remember that every other candidate will be subjected to the same treatment.

The Handshake

The first thing you must do, as you are being introduced, is shake hands. It doesn't matter whether your interviewer is male or female, or whether you're male or female; you *must* shake their hand. But does it matter how you do it?

Here's what one employer had to say about different types of handshakes, and what he thinks of them:

The limp handshake	horrible; this person is a wimp
Hot and sweaty	revolting
Half a handshake (being offered a couple of fingers)	this person lacks confidence
Too quick (hand is pulled away immediately)	disconcerting; are they scared of me?
Too long (some people simply won't let go!)	help!

The Interview Begins

And now for the next question; how firmly to squeeze! If you are a man, and your interviewer is a petite woman, be careful. Don't squeeze her hand too hard. You want her to like you, remember. She won't if you've just crushed her fingers into 5 000 pieces!

If you are a woman on the receiving end of a crushing handshake, there isn't much you can do about it except squeeze back hard. If you're worried it's going to happen again at the end of the interview, perhaps you could surreptitiously transfer any rings you're wearing to your left hand. You might also want to reconsider whether you want to work for such an inconsiderate person.

Body Language

It can be difficult to relax during an interview, but if you're still feeling extremely nervous after the first few minutes, the interviewer isn't very good at their job. They're supposed to make you feel at ease, because that's the only way they can really get to know the 'real' you.

The interviewer has a goal: to find somebody to fill the vacancy. The person most likely to fit the bill will be someone they *like*. And it's very difficult to *like* a person if they're terrified of you.

How does the interviewer know you're terrified? By your body language, of course.

- If you move about in your seat, fidget with your hair, continuously brush imaginary crumbs off your trousers – you *will* look nervous, no doubt about it. It's very difficult to have a conversation with someone who won't sit still.

- If you spend the whole interview looking out of the window – you won't only look nervous, you'll look disinterested. It is very difficult to have a conversation with someone who plainly wants to be 300 miles away.

- If you spend the whole interview looking at your watch, your interviewer will be offended. They'll think, 'How rude', and they'll be right. Doing anything other than giving them your full attention is rude.

What might help, is to remind yourself that your interviewer is just a person too. They want you to like them. They want you to be interested in them and what they have to say; it's only natural. If you can stop worrying about what they think of *you*, and concentrate on getting to know *them*, your body language will automatically stop sending 'I'm terrified' signals and send 'I'm listening and I'm interested' ones instead.

Eye Contact

Candidates who make eye contact with their interviewer are more likely to be offered the job than candidates who don't, irrespective of their suitability. Looking into the eyes of a person you've never met before is harder than you think, especially if you're feeling nervous.

Try having a conversation with a member of your family, or a friend. Talk about anything you like, but make a conscious effort to look them in the eyes all the time. The more you practice, the easier it will get.

If you're being interviewed by more than one person, try and maintain eye contact with them all.

Annoying Mannerisms

While you're getting feedback from your friends and family, ask them if you have any annoying mannerisms that irritate them. It might not be very pleasant to be told you constantly interrupt, or that you pick your nose, but it will help your interview technique no end.

Your Interviewer's Body Language

If you stop fidgeting and actually look at your interviewer, you might start noticing all the annoying little mannerisms they have. It might not occur to you that your interviewer is even more nervous than you are, but it's quite possibly the case. They *want* you to look at them. They *want* you to like them. (There is more on understanding your interviewer in Chapter 17.)

> **Note:** If you do notice some funny little habit your interviewer has, or a great big spot on the end of their nose, try and ignore it. Whatever you do, don't burst out laughing!

Swearing

Of course, you wouldn't swear in an interview would you? But plenty of people say things like, 'Gotcha', and 'OK mate'. In some situations this may be perfectly acceptable, in a formal interview room it isn't. And neither is being too familiar with the interviewer. So how are you supposed to address them?

How to Address Your Interviewer

Some organizations are young and informal, and everyone calls everyone else by their first names. Your interviewer might say, 'Hi, I'm Chris,' and if he does, you just continue to call him Chris throughout the meeting.

But what happens if he says, 'Hello, I'm Chris Brown'. Do you call him Chris, or Mr Brown? There isn't an easy answer; you really need to use your discretion. Current thinking is that you should use the surname unless he indicates otherwise. Perhaps if you feel really stuck, and 'Mr Brown' seems too formal, then consider asking, 'Can I call you Chris?' although this may feel very awkward, especially if he is a lot older than you.

The difficulty is made worse by men who insist on calling women by their first names, even though they introduce *themselves* as Mr XYZ. If this happens, you have no choice but to continue in this formal way. Whatever you do, don't call them Sir. In modern business, this level of formality is unnecessary.

Smoking

Generally, it is not a good idea to smoke during your interview. Besides, more and more companies are bringing in no-smoking policies and would much prefer to employ non-smokers. If you are a smoker, try not to do so before your interview. Non-smokers will know. It's better to try for a job in an organization you know tolerates smoking than lie about it and be found out on the first day. If that happens, you may not lose your job, but your employer will make a mental note that you lied.

Asking For a Drink

If you're very thirsty, and it doesn't look as if you're going to be offered a drink, ask for a glass of water. It's perfectly acceptable to ask, but stick to water. Never ask your interviewer to make you a cup of tea – unless they offer, of course.

Accepting a Drink

Books on interview technique always tell you not to accept a drink, but why not? If your interviewer offers you a cup of tea or coffee, the message they're giving out is 'I like you and I want you to stay and talk to me.' Believe me, if they can't stand you, they won't offer you a drink.

So I feel it is always polite to accept. I also believe that refusing gives out an 'I don't want to stay here any longer than necessary' message which you don't want to give.

If you would prefer a glass of water, don't be shy, say so. However much you are tempted, never ask for an alcoholic drink, even as a joke. Saying, 'Actually I need a stiff whisky,' may sound funny, but you'll just look desperate and nervous. When that cup of tea arrives, be appreciative. Smile and thank the person who brought it. And be careful you don't knock it over!

Going Out For a Meal

If you are booked into a hotel for two days with 25 other candidates, or simply invited out to lunch with your interviewer, there will come a point at which you have to eat. Here's a list of don'ts:

- don't order the most expensive thing on the menu;

- don't order anything messy;

- don't speak with your mouth full;

- don't complain, be appreciative instead;

- and finally, don't drink so much you can't stand up afterwards!

Claiming Expenses: a Warning

You may be offered travel expenses, ie reimbursement of the money you spent travelling to the interview. If you came by train or bus, keep the receipts just in case. Never claim for more than you spent.

Also, watch out! I know of one person who, when asked to sign for bus and train fares, failed to notice a deliberate error in the addition – a rather underhand trick, but then she was applying for an accounting job. Needless to say, she was unsuccessful.

16 Key Questions You Will Be Asked

These are the most popular questions you will be faced with, and some of them look really tough. Using the research you've carried out, think about how you would answer them *before* you're put under the spotlight.

But don't just think about the answers in relation to your job-hunt. Think about them for yourself too.

Why Are the Answers Important to Me?

Some of these questions, especially the ones relating to goals and ambitions are things that perhaps you could think about, not just in terms of persuading an employer to hire you, but for your whole life.

What *are* your goals? What do you want to be doing in 5, or even 10 years' time? Will working for this company put you on the right road to achieving this?

Unfortunately, too many people just fall into the first job (or the first career) that comes along and it takes years before they realize that they'd much rather be doing something completely different. And too many people never come to this realization; they just remain unhappy without really knowing why.

Finally, when thinking about how to answer these questions, be honest with yourself. There's no point preparing answers that are completely untrue, or that paint a totally false picture. Remember that if successful, this will be the very beginning of a long, healthy, working relationship with the people asking the questions.

The Most Popular Questions

'Why do you want to work for this company?'

Depend upon it – you *will* be asked this. Luckily it's the sort of question you can prepare for. If you've researched the company, and the job itself, it should be easy to give a convincing answer (and a truthful one) about why you want the job. So think about it. Why *do* you want to work for them?

Apart from your honest reasons for wanting to work for that specific organization, a little bit of flattery will also go a long way. 'Well, I've found out that in this industry, you are the market leader. I want to work for a company which is very successful, and I know I could contribute to your success.'

Of course, once you've said something like that, you're opening yourself up to all sorts of questions. How did you research their company exactly? What else did you find out? How exactly can you contribute to their success? But they're going to ask you those questions anyway. Don't kid yourself they're not.

'Why do you want this job?'

Saying something like, 'I need the money,' is no good. You need to stick to reasons which demonstrate how interested, and how suitable you are for the job. Do you have any particular skills which you can bring to the job? What aspects of the job seem exciting to you? Try and prepare your answer to this before you get to interview.

'Why would you be good at this job?'

Again, finding out as much as you can about the job before you get to interview, will help you answer this one. You need to match your skills to the job specification. And it isn't enough to simply list your qualifications. Personal qualities are equally important when it comes to finding someone who will do the job really well.

For instance, a school looking for a reception teacher would expect candidates to be suitably qualified, but would naturally prefer a candidate who loves children and has loads of energy and patience.

'Why should we employ you over anyone else?'

This is a bit of a nasty question, but it can be overcome by identifying some of your particular characteristics and thinking about how they apply to the job in question. Being able to 'do the job' is not enough. For instance, if you are going for a technical job then it's a good bet that the other applicants will be technically competent. Most of them will be able to perform just as well as you, or even better.

The interviewer knows that. What they don't know is what *else* you have to offer. What makes you special? To answer this question satisfactorily, you need to come up with some 'extras'. How about something like this: 'Well, apart from being able to handle this job from a technical point of view, I work very well under pressure. I'm used to organizing and prioritizing my work which, from what you've told me about the deadlines you have to meet, will be vital for this job.'

'How do you rate yourself against your contemporaries?'

The answer to this question depends to some extent upon who is interviewing you, and what their own position is in the organization. If it's the managing director, they might be looking for confidence and a certainty that you're good at your job. If your interviewer is going to be a colleague, saying you are better than everyone else may sound not only arrogant, but threatening as well.

'How do your contemporaries perceive you?'

Try and pick out your best and most distinctive qualities, and always be honest. Don't ignore the qualities which would be good ones to have for the job. For instance, if you're talking to a company which organizes exhibitions, you could say, 'I think my contemporaries would say I am a people person. They would probably say I have a very good memory for names and faces, and that I'm a good organizer.'

'What are your strengths and weaknesses?'

Obviously the strengths you can tailor to the sort of characteristics you know the interviewer is looking for, but what about the weaknesses? You need to be a bit careful. Don't try and be funny. Saying, 'I'm useless at getting up in the morning,' won't go down too well at all.

How about saying something like, 'Well, I think that sometimes I can be too disciplined for my own good. Sometimes I need to relax and have more fun.' You can see what I'm getting at; make the weaknesses look like strengths in disguise.

'Where do you see yourself in five years' time?'

Another case of considering what your interviewer wants to hear. If they are the managing director, ambition may be encouraged. But if your interviewer is going to be a colleague or your boss, they might perceive an ambition to be promoted as quickly as possible as a threat.

The last thing they'll want to do is to hire someone who will compete with them from the word go. Telling them that your intention is to get as much experience as possible in this particular area might be a more diplomatic response.

On the other hand, if they work for a completely different department, such as personnel, they may not care what you say as long as you sound convincing.

'What are your goals?'

Again, 'your goals' (or the ones you're about to tell them, anyway) should be tailored to the job. For instance, if you want to work in the caring professions, you could say you are aiming to

'Make a difference. I really want to help other people. Also, I want to be able to develop my knowledge so that I can become a really skilled practitioner.'

'What sort of salary are you looking for?'

If the salary isn't advertised, you could very well be asked this question. So how should you answer? You don't want to undervalue yourself, and you don't want to price yourself out of the market. In this situation, diplomacy is needed. 'Well, I expect to be paid what I'm worth, as a minimum around the... mark, but for the right job I may be willing to accept less.'

Even better, turn the question round altogether and ask, 'What sort of salary are you offering?'

On the subject of salaries it pays to have researched the market. Lots of ideas as to how to do this in Chapter 1.

Commitment Related Questions

You can see these questions coming a mile off, but the good thing about them is that you can think about the answers now. The fact that they are asked at all, will give you a clue as to what it's going to be like working for this particular organization. For instance: 'How do you feel about working long hours?' or 'How do you feel about working weekends?'

Before you assure your interviewer that you absolutely love working non-stop, think about it. It doesn't take a genius to work out that anyone who asks this question, will probably be expecting you to ditch your social life, at least some of the time.

Probably the best thing to do is avoid answering the question directly. Ask your own question instead. 'I don't mind working long hours when the pressure's on, but can you give me an idea of the sort of thing you're talking about?'

That way, you get a clear picture of exactly what you're letting yourself in for. If you're quite happy, make sure they know it. If you're not, discuss your reservations and be honest.

Key Questions You Will Be Asked

'How are you going to cope with the change from school/university?'

This is a good question. If you're coming straight from school or university, how *are* you going to cope with the change? Have you thought about it? It can be difficult to make the transition from full-time education to full-time employment, and now your job is to convince your interviewer that you are capable of it.

Admit that you realize it's going to be hard (implying that you've given the matter serious consideration) and then go on to say that you know you have the self-discipline and that you are ready to make a long-term commitment.

Also, if you've had any sort of work experience, even part-time or holiday work, voluntary or charity work, now is the time to talk about it. Your interviewer will be impressed, and also reassured that you are mature enough to make the grade.

So whatever you say, make sure it isn't, 'I haven't the foggiest idea.' See Chapter 10 for the sort of thing you could be asked about your leisure interests.

Competency Related Questions

Questions based upon a person's ability to do the job and fit into the organization are very popular. Within the recruitment business, the jargon is 'competency'. Large organizations even give their interviewers ready-made dictionaries of questions based upon different 'competencies' such as business awareness, customer focus, working with others and self-motivation. Here are some examples.

'Describe a situation where you had to listen very carefully to someone.' 'Describe a situation where you had to deal with a particularly angry person.'

With these two questions, if you substitute the word 'customer' for 'someone' and 'person', it's easy to see what the interviewer is getting at. 'How are you going to deal with my customers?' is what you're being asked.

'Tell me about a situation when you had to cope with a particularly demanding task.'

With this example, the interviewer wants to find out how self-motivated you are. It isn't really the situation that the interviewer is interested in, it's what you did to ensure you coped with it that they really want to hear about.

'Describe the last time you missed a deadline.'

This question is about taking responsibility for your actions. The interviewer wants to know why the situation occurred, how responsible you were for it, and most importantly, what you did to try and overcome the problem.

'What do you know about our competitors?'

This question, in one form or another, is asked all the time. If you've done your research, you should be able to satisfy your interviewer that you do possess some business awareness, and why you've chosen *them* above their competition.

'What techniques and tools do you use to manage your time and plan?'

If you are an organized person, you'll already be using a number of strategies to plan and organize your work/study/personal schedule. Using lists, keeping a diary, prioritizing tasks and tackling the most important ones first, are all 'time management' skills. Your interviewer wants to know if you have them.

'Describe the last time you had to analyse a lot of

information or data.'

Apart from wanting to know what was involved, your interviewer wants to know how you analysed the information, and what you learnt from the experience.

'Tell me about a time when you worked as part of a team.'

Questions about teams are common. If you're not the athletic type, don't panic. It's not about sport. It's about your ability to work with other people. It's about sharing information and working with others towards a common goal, rather than in isolation. It's about making a positive contribution and supporting others.

'What behaviours do you consider key for a successful manager?'

You could easily be asked this, in one guise or another, when you go for managerial or trainee manager jobs. Obviously you'll need to talk about being enthusiastic, being interested in the people working for you, setting realistic targets, making expectations clear, giving and receiving feedback, being a good communicator, and so on. All the attributes you hope your new boss will have!

Trick Questions

These sort of questions require some thought. I've called them 'trick questions', not because the interviewer is trying to trip you up, but because the most obvious answer isn't always enough to satisfy them.

What happens is that the interviewer will describe an imaginary situation and then ask how *you* would deal with it. Here's an example: You are working on an important project with a tight deadline, and you come up against a problem. This problem is so difficult, and so time-consuming, you know you won't be able to meet the deadline without working all night and all weekend. What would you do?

Most people would simply say, 'I'd work harder', or 'I'd put in the extra hours over the weekend.' That wouldn't be the wrong answer, but it wouldn't be the right one either. What is being looked for is a more creative response, something that shows your ability to find the best possible solution. This is what you could say:

> Well first of all I would consult my manager to find out whether the problem could be avoided altogether, or at the very least, put aside until after the deadline. If not, I would find out if there was any possibility of the deadline being put back. If this wasn't possible then I would find out if there was anyone else available to help me. If all else failed, I would put in the extra hours to ensure the project was completed on time.

Here's another example: a customer asks you for a product that isn't available. What would you do? Most people would answer by saying they would apologize to the customer. What else could they do?

A better answer would be: 'I would check whether the product was really unavailable, or just temporarily out of stock. If temporarily out of stock, I'd offer to order the item for the customer. If the product really was unavailable, I'd do my best to offer an alternative.'

These questions are tricky because they are devised to test how creatively and logically you think. If you don't have a creative or logical bone in your body, you won't be able to see beyond the most obvious solution. However, forewarned is forearmed.

What if I Don't Understand the Question?

Asking, 'Do you mean…' or 'Are you referring to…' is much better than waffling. It may also encourage your interviewer to rephrase the question. If you've already answered, you can always say, 'Does that answer your question?' If you've already answered the question, you can ask 'Was that okay, or were you getting at something else?'

Checking to make sure you have understood something, or that someone has understood you, is a management skill so don't be afraid to use it.

What if I Can't Think of an Answer?

Take your time. It's better to take a moment or two to consider your answer (and what your interviewer is really getting at) than jump in quick with an off-the-cuff remark. You can always say, 'Hmm, I think I need a few seconds to think about that one', before you answer. Make time for yourself. Pausing like this is always perfectly acceptable. It also gives the impression that you're taking things seriously.

I remember once saying, 'I knew you were going to ask me that question, and I'm afraid I just haven't got an answer.' Of course, you can only say that once!

Questions They're Not Allowed to Ask

Organizations are always declaring that they are 'equal opportunity employers' – and so they have to be if they want to comply with employment legislation. Part of being an equal opportunity employer is the commitment to treat job applicants fairly, and not discriminate on the basis of gender, race or disability.

This policy is supposed to extend the entire way through the recruitment process, including advertisements, selection procedures and questions asked at interview. Every employer is fully aware of the sort of questions they're not supposed to ask. But that doesn't mean they won't ask.

Sexual Discrimination

If you are young, female and single; be prepared for one of these questions to pop up at least once during your job hunt: 'Do you have a boyfriend?' or 'Do you have any plans to get married in the near future?'

Basically, your interviewer is trying to find out when you plan to have children and leave (and reject you on that basis). Unfortunately, there are still a few people around who believe that the only thing a woman wants to do is to get married, have children and stop working.

However much you're tempted, don't say 'Hey, mind your own business.' Even though you know full well they shouldn't have asked, you'll be dismissed as being rude and aggressive.

Whatever your plans are, best to tell your interviewer something along the lines of, 'No. I want to develop my career, and enjoy all the benefits of working. I really haven't got any plans to settle down at all.' Besides it's true: you wouldn't be applying for jobs in the first place if you didn't want to work.

In fact, there are plenty of employers who, despite firmly believing that any 23-year-old woman they take on will leave within five years to raise a family, would still prefer to hire a 23-year-old woman than any other candidate. So be polite and reassure them, and then get on with the rest of the interview.

If you are young, female and married, you may be asked: 'Do you have any children?' If the answer is no, the next question may be: 'Have you got any plans to start a family?' Your answer should be something similar to the one given above. Again, better to tell the interviewer what they want to hear, than be rude.

If you do have children, the next question is pretty obvious: 'What childcare arrangements do you have?' The interviewer wants to know whether you have someone reliable to look after your children while you work, or whether you're going to have to take a lot of time off. To a certain extent, I think this is a reasonable question to ask. The way it's phrased could be seen to discriminate because it assumes that because you are a woman, you must be the parent responsible for childcare.

However, there may not be any ulterior motive for asking the question at all. An increasing number of employers offer childcare facilities, and your interviewer may simply be trying to find out if you wish to use them.

The best thing to do is answer the question honestly. After all, if you do have children, you are going to have to have made arrangements to have them looked after while you work. Again, don't say, 'That's none of your business.'

If you are male, and the working environment of the organization you have applied to is female dominated, you could be asked something like this: 'Would you find it difficult, not having other men to work with?' or 'How do you feel about a female boss?' Obviously, it would not be a good idea to say, 'Actually I've always been terrified of women', unless you made it plain that it was a complete joke and that of course you would be quite happy to have a female boss. Best to say it would be quite delightful!

Discrimination Against People With Disability

If you are disabled then be prepared for questions relating to your disability, such as: 'What does your disability prevent you from doing?' or 'Would your disability mean you need to take a lot of time off work?'

Employers are supposed to concentrate on your abilities, not your disabilities. They are not supposed to make assumptions about what you can and can't do, or assume that you would be a health and safety risk, or that you'd take more time off work than anyone else – in fact research shows the opposite to be true.

That doesn't mean they are not allowed to ask questions that focus on your ability to do the job. Reassure the interviewer that you don't foresee any problems at all. The best thing to do is to answer honestly, and with good humour and not say, 'I don't see why I should answer that.'

Racial Discrimination

It would be discriminatory not to employ someone because of his or her religious commitments or race, but candidates are still occasionally questioned on the subject. This doesn't necessarily mean that the organization itself has a policy of race discrimination. Most discrimination that occurs at interview comes from the interviewer's own personal prejudices, rather than the organization's.

Remember that if your interviewer is from the personnel department, you may never come up against them again. On the other hand, if your interviewer is your possible new boss, perhaps you should think hard about whether you still want the job.

Whatever you say, be polite and courteous. Reassure the interviewer that you don't foresee any problems at all, answer honestly, and with good humour. Do not say, 'I don't see why I should answer that', or 'That's a racist question' even if you'd like to stand up and punch them on the nose.

17 Games Interviewers Play

Most of us automatically assume that the people who interview us know their stuff. We assume that they have the skill and knowledge to do their jobs properly but the reality can often be very different.

The vast majority of interviewers have never been trained in the task. They've never been given any guidance on what questions to ask or how to get the most out of the person they're interviewing. That's the first preconceived idea that needs throwing out of the window; the belief that your interviewer knows what they're doing.

The second idea people have about interviewers is that they enjoy interviewing people. Don't they just love the feeling of power that being in the driving seat gives them? Well this may be true for some, but for the majority the opposite is more likely to be the case.

How is Your Interviewer Feeling?

They're nervous

While *you* are shaking like a jelly, *they'll* be worried about the impression they're making on you. Amazing but true. Increase your chances of being hired by making your interviewer think you like them, and that you're impressed by what they're saying.

They're confused

There's no doubt about it, interviewing people one after another is very confusing. After four or five people, even the most experienced interviewer is starting to get muddled up. It's easy to remember which candidate came in blind drunk, but as to the rest, who knows.

Even top recruitment professionals acknowledge the difficulty in remembering which candidate is which. They've even invented their own terminology for the condition: the 'primacy effect' means remembering the first candidates and forgetting the later ones, and the 'recency effect' means, yes you guessed it, remembering the later candidates and forgetting the first ones.

If top professionals are prone to the condition, what hope for the run-of-the-mill interviewer. The only way to combat confusion is to take notes. If your interviewer takes notes, be grateful. If they don't bother, consider handing them another copy of your CV. Consider writing or telephoning them after the interview; anything in fact to jog their memory and make sure, even if they forget all the other candidates, they remember *you*.

They're worried

What could they possibly have to worry about? Quite a lot, in fact. The most awful thing for any interviewer is that at the end of the day they have to make a decision, and what if they get it wrong? What if the person they pick turns out to be totally unsuitable? What will happen if they make the wrong choice? If they do, then they will get the blame.

If your interviewer is the managing director, they'll be even more worried. They'll be fully aware of the consequences of choosing the wrong person. They'll know full well the disruption, the wasted time and the great cost of having to go through the recruitment process all over again.

Picking the wrong person isn't the only thing that concerns interviewers. If they are going to be a colleague, or even your immediate boss, they might be worrying about:

- whether you'll fit into the department;
- whether you'll be a nice person to have around;
- whether you'll pose a threat to them – will you outshine them?
- will you end up earning more than they do?
- will you end up being promoted over their head?

Obviously, if you understand where your interviewer is coming from, you've more chance of landing the job.

Is There Anyone Who Won't Be Concerned About My Ambition?

Generally, personnel department staff will not be too concerned about how ambitious you are; after all, you won't be competing with them, will you? They're more likely to concentrate on finding staff with the required level of ability (and also reaching their recruitment targets).

The owners of a business, and senior executives will also be more likely to look upon ambition with approval. They want to employ high-flyers. They want to employ people who express a desire to do well. They know that the more successful their employees are, the more successful their company will be as a whole.

What if I Can't Work Out Where My Interviewer Stands?

In this case, listen hard. Do they refer to the organization as 'we', or do they refer to it by name? An interviewer who talks about the organization very enthusiastically and uses the word 'we', many times, for example, 'We have 10 sales offices,' and 'This is the way we like things done around here', may be quite amenable to ambitious new recruits.

Conversely, an interviewer who refers to the company by name, as if they are an outsider, may unconsciously think of themselves as occupying a subordinate role and resent ambition.

Games Interviewers Play

It takes all sorts to make a world, and some of them end up interviewing!

The Quiet Ones

They don't say a lot. They just sit back, ask lots of open-ended questions and let you get on with it. So when do you stop talking? In general, try and answer each question fully, but don't talk for more than a couple of minutes at the most. Prompt them for feedback by saying things like, 'Does that answer your question?' or, 'Do you want me to go into more detail?' or, 'Is that enough information?'

The Friendly Ones

On the surface, an ideal interviewer to have. They're friendly, welcoming, and make you feel at ease straight away. In fact, they're so friendly, you could even be forgiven for thinking that they want to be your best friend.

But be warned. It's easy to be lulled into such a false sense of security that you start saying things you shouldn't. When you feel relaxed, it's easy to be flippant, use bad language or be rude about other people. Don't. Remember you are being interviewed, and act in a professional manner all the time.

The Confused Ones

Already covered a little bit in this chapter, these interviewers have seen lots of candidates and forgotten to make any notes, so by the time you arrive they're really muddled. Perhaps they've only just been handed your CV, or even worse, they've lost it and haven't a clue as to who's about to walk through the door.

As well as doing all you can to remind this interviewer who you are, eg, giving them a copy of your CV and following the interview up with a telephone call, it's your job to make them feel your presence in the office would be a godsend and the answer to all their problems. How did they ever manage without you?

The Inexperienced Ones

Even worse than the type described above, this type has no idea how to conduct an interview, and usually spends the entire time talking about themselves. The great temptation is to sit there and let them do the talking, but don't. They'll never remember you afterwards. The only thing you can do is turn their inexperience to your advantage by taking the initiative and asking all the questions, and then answering them!

For instance, 'Who would I be working with?' would certainly elicit some sort of answer, say, working with five other people on the same project. You then say something like, 'That's great. I want to work closely with other people and I've always done my best work in a team.' Asked and answered!

The other thing the inexperienced type does, is forget to tell the office that anyone's coming in. So the moment you sit down, the telephone rings. Two minutes later there's another interruption, and this continues the whole time.

The only way to deal with this is to stay calm and convince yourself you really do have the patience of a saint. On a more practical note, getting your notebook out and jotting down the last thing that was said before you were interrupted, will ensure you remember what you were talking about and make you appear super efficient in the process.

The Professional Ones

A 'professional' interviewer will be the one to give you the hardest time. This type believes that skilful questioning is the only way to achieve a productive interview, and of course, they're right. Often they keep an interview checklist right in front of them just to make sure they don't forget anything.

Generally they begin with easy, innocuous questions. Just as you are beginning to relax, they move up a level to the 'when', 'where', 'what', and 'why', questions which require you to do a lot more talking and explaining.

Then they progress to the very complex questions, the ones where they ask what you'd do in certain hypothetical situations. See Chapter 16 on how to deal effectively with this, because sometimes the most obvious answer isn't the one they're looking for.

This probing, all encompassing technique will leave you drained, but stay cool and remember that asking your own intelligent, relevant questions and sounding enthusiastic is the best way to handle the situation.

The Aggressive Ones

Luckily, the days of the 'stress' interview are coming to an end. Most reputable organizations do not encourage their staff to upset potential new recruits for three very good reasons.

- You can get more information out of a candidate by making them feel comfortable and treating them with respect.

- The way potential new recruits are treated reflects on the organization as a whole.

- Legislation forbids the asking of unfair questions relating to sex, race or disability (but see Chapter 16 for more information on this).

If you do get an interviewer who is rude or aggressive, or who asks you a lot of personal questions, which are none of their business, ask yourself, 'Do I really want to work for somebody like this?'

18 Even More Successful Interview Techniques

This chapter is about the things you can do to change a dithering interviewer into an enthusiastic one. Enthusiastic about you, that is.

Convince Your Interviewer That You Really Want the Job

Your interviewer has a goal: to fill the vacancy. Ideally, they will be looking for someone who is not only capable of doing the job, but also who wants the job.

Finding somebody who *wants* the job is just as important (if not more so) than identifying a person who can 'do it'. For the employer, the reasons are simple. Here are just a few of them. A person who *wants* the job will be:

- more reliable and actually turn up every day;
- be less likely to leave;
- be more likely to do a good job.

You can see it makes sense to give your interviewer as many reasons as possible for *wanting* the job. Here are just a few suggestions, and they are all valid reasons why you might really want a particular job.

It sounds really interesting

You can't really say that a job sounds fantastic with any conviction until you've found out quite a lot about it, so ask lots of questions about what the job entails. If the job does sound interesting, say so, and say why.

It is going to employ skills you want to use

Again, you need to know quite a lot about the actual job before you can tell the interviewer that you enjoy using those skills, so ask questions.

You know the organization is a good one to work for

This requires you to have done your homework. Perhaps you've discovered the organization is the market leader in its field and you want to work for them because you can see they are very successful. Perhaps they have a very good reputation, or you've heard they treat their staff like royalty, or that they believe in developing staff through training. If so, say so.

The job is perfect for you in terms of location, hours, etc

Perhaps the most important thing to you is being able to walk to work. Perhaps the hours suit your lifestyle perfectly. If so, say so.

The job is going to involve doing things you enjoy

Do you think you are going to enjoy doing the job? If the answer is yes, say so and why.

There's no doubt about it, organizations want to employ people who can commute without any hassle and who enjoy the work. They're more likely to work hard, more likely to do a good job, and much less likely to leave.

In every case, if you can find reasons to tell your interviewer why you really want the job, you must do so. But one word of warning, *wanting* the job is not the same as *needing* the job. See under the heading 'Things that turn employers off immediately' for some examples. Make sure your reasons for wanting the job are all things which will benefit the organization, not just yourself.

Turn the Interview into a Conversation

Too many people go into an interview, sit and listen, but say nothing. As one employer put it, 'It's like having a conversation with myself.'

You have to give the person who is interviewing you some sign that you have understood what they've said, and that you are actually interested. Sitting there staring into space is not the way to do it.

It's not difficult to convince the interviewer that you are listening. Maintaining eye contact and a nod from time to time, saying 'Yes', and 'I understand', is all it takes. Other things you can say are, 'That sounds good', or 'I like the sound of that', and, 'Does that mean...' followed by a relevant question. These techniques all demonstrate that you understand what's being said. In other words, don't just sit there and be 'interviewed', have a conversation.

Responding to the interviewer and asking relevant questions will give them the feedback they are looking for. Unless they feel confident that you understand what's been said, there isn't any way they can offer you a job. To emphasize the point, too many people just sit there and say nothing. Sadly, they never get offered the job. The interviewer just doesn't know if anything's gone in.

Ask Questions

Before you get to the interview you should have made a list of all the things you wanted to find out about the organization, and the job itself (over and above what you have already found out, of course). You have a right to find out as much as you can, after all it will be *you* doing it, every day, week after week, month after month. You can put the list in your briefcase and even bring it out during the interview. No one is going to object to you saying, 'I had a list of things I wanted to know. I just want to make sure I've covered everything.'

So what do you want to know? Here are several suggestions that you might like to try. The answers you get should provide a valuable insight into the working of the organization, as well as giving you a chance to relax while your interviewer does all the work.

'Suppose I get the job, can you describe a typical day?'

Listen closely to the answer. Does this sound like the sort of thing you want to do? If it does, say so. 'That sounds great. I particularly like the idea of...'

'What are the best and the worst things about working here?'

This one really puts them on the spot, but as long as you ask in a non-aggressive and friendly way, you will appear interested and truly serious. It also turns the whole interview round. You'll find that instead of having to sell yourself to them, your prospective employer will start selling the job to you! Again, give your interviewer feedback. Aim to sound enthusiastic about the good things, and positive about the bad things, 'Well, that's okay. I think I can handle that.'

If you're too chicken to ask the interviewer, try asking one of your prospective new colleagues, if you get a chance to meet them. Remember to be enthusiastic and positive with them too. Don't say, 'That's terrible. How do you put up with it?', whatever you're actually thinking.

'Who will I be working with? Is there a chance that I can get to meet them?'

Don't be scared to ask this. The more contact you have with other employees, the more chance you have of being offered the job. Besides, you do want to meet them, don't you?

Again, when your interviewer talks about the people you'll be working with, give feedback, tailored to the information you've been given. For instance, 'That's great, I much prefer to work in a small office', or 'That's great, I like being one of a large team.'

'I read in your literature that you... Can you explain how...?'

Asking questions that show you have done some homework can only impress a prospective employer. It also gives them a chance to talk about their organizations, which they all love doing.

'I know you do... but can you tell me about the specific work your department does?'

Another example of you showing off your knowledge of the organization and your interest in it. Remember, the vast majority of candidates will have no idea what the organization does. With these two last questions, you will have had to do some research *before* you get to the interview, but there's no point doing all that work and then not using it to your advantage.

'What sort of on-the-job training can I expect?'

Many companies pride themselves on being able to offer their staff all sorts of personal development plans. What you want to know is, is this company one of them? Will you be encouraged to further your career by studying/taking professional exams? If this is what you want, now is the time to find out what's available. Once you've started the job, it's too late.

'What are the potential possibilities for career progression?'

You need to be a bit careful with this one. Appearing to be *too* ambitious may not have the desired effect. A lot depends upon your interviewer's role in the organization (see Chapter 17 for more tips on handling this dilemma).

Having said this be careful, most interviewers do expect you to ask this question. In fact, they're hoping you will, because it's the one thing for which they have a ready prepared answer. Listen closely. Is it a frank and full description of how people progress up the career ladder, or is it a lot of waffle followed by a quick side-step round the subject? If you are ambitious, *now* is the time to find out. Again, once you've started the job, it's too late.

And while I'm on the subject of career progression, beware of the manager in a tiny little company who stresses how wonderful the promotion prospects are. Think about it: the only chances of you getting promoted are if he (or she) leaves!

What Not to Ask

Generally, employers expect you to ask questions. They want you to. They want to be given an opportunity to talk all about themselves and their companies, and they want you to be interested in them. So, as a general rule, if you want to know, ask.

However, always stick to questions that indicate your interest in the job itself and the organization. Leave the 'What am I going to get out of it' questions until you feel confident that they really do want you. By this, I mean things like, 'What salary are you offering?' and 'How much holiday will I get?'

The other kind of questions that should not be asked are bad ones! If your questions are relevant and intelligent, then they will reflect well on you. Asking loads of questions just for the sake of it (which many candidates do) will have the opposite effect.

What Happens if I Ask Too Many Questions?

If you've made your interviewer do all the work, there's always a chance that they might suddenly lean forward and say, 'Hey, who's doing the interviewing, you or me?' If this happens, just laugh in a good-natured way and let them do a bit of the talking. Let them take control of the interview, at least for a while! Don't ever worry about asking too much, it's far, far better than keeping quiet.

Candidates who don't ask any questions run the risk of being seen as boring, even downright stupid. Their success rate in the job-hunting stakes is always minimal. Would you offer a job to someone who didn't want to know anything about it?

Make Notes

It is a good idea to have a pen and notebook ready so you can jot down one or two things the interviewer tells you. It shows them that you are taking the process seriously, and that you are listening to what they've said – and you think it's so important you want to write it down.

Jotting down a few notes can have a practical purpose as well. If you walk into the room and find more than one person waiting to interview you, it's a good idea, once you've found out who they are, to write their names down. Don't worry about spelling their names correctly at this stage. Only you will know what's written on your notepad. You can always speak to the receptionist on your way out, or ring up later and ask for the correct spelling.

Knowing who these people are will prove very useful if you are invited back for a second interview. You'll be able to walk straight in and say, 'Mr Phillips, it's good to see you again.' He'll be so impressed, he'll conduct the rest of the interview in a rosy glow.

One word of warning. Use your notebook sparingly. Having somebody scribbling away the whole time can be very distracting for the interviewer. They won't know if you're interested in what they're saying, or practising for a shorthand exam.

Smile

It's a well known fact that candidates who smile are more likely to be offered the job than candidates who don't. Strange but true.

Make Eye Contact

Another truism is that candidates who look into their interviewers eyes are much more likely to be offered the job than candidates who don't. Would you hire someone who didn't look at you?

Ask For Your Interviewer's Business Card

If you haven't written your interviewer's name down, you can still get the information at the end by asking for their business card. Just say, 'Have you got a business card you could give me?' Whatever you do, leave out 'Because I can't remember your name.'

Asking for a person's business card creates a good impression anyway because you're telling them you recognize they have sufficient status to possess such a thing in the first place.

Meeting Other Employees: How to Behave

Many companies, knowing candidates will be on their best behaviour when they come along for an interview, employ strategies to find out what sort of person you *really* are. The way they do this is to take you out of the formal atmosphere of the interview room and into a situation, which is far more relaxed, or so it seems. A member of staff may take you on a guided tour, introducing you to other members of staff and generally chat you up in the process. You may be invited to spend a little time with the people with whom you are going to be working, you may even be invited out for lunch (unlikely, but you never know!)

There isn't anything sinister about any of this. Your potential employer simply wants to find out what sort of person you are and whether the existing members of staff like you. If they do, their enthusiasm will probably land you the job. If you're rude, or treat anyone in an offhand way, the chances of you being offered the job are remote, however well the actual interview went.

Not only must you be polite and friendly in this relaxed atmosphere, you also have to be careful what you say. It's easy to be caught off guard when you're feeling relaxed. So don't tell the canteen staff that you've just been interviewed by Godzilla, because Godzilla will surely hear about it!

Ask For the Order

Going back to the actual interview for a moment, asking for the order really means asking for the job. If you are applying for a job in any sort of sales capacity, you will be expected to do this, as a matter of course. But you can do it for any job. Asking for the order simply means asking questions, usually towards the tail end of the interview, about how well you've done, and what your chances are. Besides, you're dying to know anyway.

'Is there anything I can do, or anything I can tell you, which might influence your decision?' is a good one. It shows you want the job

Landing Your First Job

and it shows you are willing to do more to get it. What you're really saying is, 'Do you know enough about me to offer me the job?'

'Can you give me any feedback as to my chances at this stage?' This is where you are likely to find out where you stand and how many other candidates are yet to be interviewed. You might be told, 'We've seen 10 people so far, and you're in the top three,' in which case the next thing to say might be something like: 'That's great. I want you to know that I really want this job.'

Don't be shy. Don't feel that saying something like this might be seen as pushy. Your interviewer wants to find someone who really wants the job. Your interviewer wants to be reassured that they have made the right choice. Make it easy for them and tell them what they want to hear.

You can try this technique on any other employees you get to meet. If you get the opportunity, tell them something positive about your interview, how interesting the job sounded and how much you want it.

'What happens now? Do you still have a lot of people to see?' is the same sort of thing. Asking this question should elicit some useful information, such as for how long the interviewer thinks the interviews will continue. If you're told, 'I've got another week of interviews left,' you'll have a better idea when to ring and ask how your application is progressing. 'Did you have a huge number of people apply for this job?' It isn't really an 'ask for the order' question, but it shows interest and might spark off a good conversation.

Finally, as the interview is brought to a close, stay friendly and appreciative. 'Thank you very much for your time. I hope to be meeting you again very soon,' and another warm handshake, can only create a good impression.

Note: More on asking for the order in Chapter 20.

Things that Turn Employers off Immediately

- Don't emphasize how kind they are to have granted you this interview, you'll just sound desperate.

- Don't stress how much you 'need' the job because of your dire financial situation, you'll just sound sad and unable to cope with life.

- Don't complain about your school/college/university/current boss. Complaining about your current situation will just make you look difficult to please. Organizations take on people that they think they can please. They know that if their employees are happy, they'll do a better job. People who spend the entire interview grumbling always get rejected.

- Don't talk about failure. Don't tell the interviewer about your exam failures, your relationship failures, your sacking from the part-time job you held last summer.

- Don't try and score points at the expense of your interviewer. Treat them as equals. Never give them the impression that you think they're an imbecile (even if they are).

- Never be rude, or act in an arrogant or conceited manner. Don't say, 'You've already asked me that' in a voice that makes it quite clear you think they're an idiot.

- Don't swear. Even if your interviewer does, resist the temptation to join in.

Explaining Previous Bad Work Experiences

Although this book is primarily for people who are looking for their first job, many of you will have already had a taste of employment, be it as part of a sandwich course, work experience or other part-time (or even full-time) employment. If the experience wasn't a good one, don't highlight the fact by trying to be clever. What you're really saying when you say, 'We had a personality clash,' is 'They couldn't stand me'.

Similarly, 'We had a difference in opinion', will be interpreted as, 'I was wrong but I wasn't prepared to admit it' and 'I didn't like the direction the company was going' can only be translated as 'They didn't think I was promotion material'.

Organizations want to take on winners, so act like one.

19 Afterwards

As far as you are concerned, the assessment process is at an end. You've got no more interviews to attend, no more forms to fill in, no more questionnaires to struggle through. Nothing to do but wait and see.

Actually, doing nothing is only one of your options. It's certainly the least likely to land you the job. If you're thinking, 'What else could I possibly do?' there are a number of things that could tip the scales in your favour.

Be True to Yourself

Perhaps the first thing to do is think about whether you want to try and tip the scales in your favour. Do you still want the job? At this stage in the game, it's always a good idea to sit back and reflect a little.

- Think about the recruitment process that you've just been through. How were you treated? With respect? With professionalism?

- Think about the organization itself. Is it the sort of place you'd love to work, or does the prospect fill you with dread? Are the people friendly and welcoming, or are they the sort you'd cross the street to avoid?

- Think about the job itself? Did they answer your questions satisfactorily? Does it still look as good as you first thought?

If the answer is 'no', then go back and start again. Consider your options, follow up other leads, continue to apply for other jobs. Perhaps it would be a good idea to examine what you really do want out of a job. Was it just this particular organization that you didn't like, or should you be considering a completely different career? If the answer is 'not sure' then try and weigh up the pros and cons. Writing them down often helps.

If your answer is 'yes', then read on.

Tracking Your Application

If you have applied to a large company, they will probably be able to track your application. They'll be able to tell you (if you forgot to ask during your interview) how many more people are due to be interviewed, and whether you are still in the running. All you have to do is call them up and ask.

If you applied to a smaller company and you haven't heard anything within a reasonable time, don't wait for them to call you; you call them.

Ask For Feedback

The burning question, now the interviewing process is over, is 'How did I do?' Not many applicants ever ask for feedback. If you ask, the organization will know that you are serious. They are also likely to give you the feedback you want. If you can combine asking about how you did, with telling them how much you want the job, it can only improve your chances of success. More ideas on asking for feedback in Chapter 21.

> **Tip:** Make sure you are always polite, friendly and appreciative when you ask for feedback. If you are aggressive, you won't get anywhere.

More Ideas on What to Say

'I've thought about the things we discussed at our meeting, and I wanted to tell you that I really do want this job.'

Imagine you are doing the hiring. You have two equally good candidates to choose from. After the interviews are over, one of them contacts you and says how enthusiastic he or she is about the job and how much they want it. The other candidate does nothing. You never hear from them again. Which one would you choose?

'I've thought about the things we discussed at our meeting, and the more I think about them, the more I know I could do a great job for you.'

Again, imagine you are doing the hiring. After the interviews, one candidate does nothing, the other rings up and tells you how enthusiastic he or she is about the job and how good they know they're going to be. Which one would you choose?

It's obvious, isn't it? If you were doing the hiring, you'd like to be reassured that you've made the right decision. You'd like to give the job to someone who really wants the job and believes they can do it well.

Reassuring the Employer: Why it's so Important

The person whose job it is to hire people is a person too. They want to make sure they make the right decision. They want to make the right decision because:

- it's very time consuming and expensive to hire people. The decision needs to be the right one, the first time round;

- if they make the right decision, they'll get some of the credit;

- if they make the wrong decision, they'll get all the blame.

However good the candidate is on paper, however wonderfully they performed in the interview; there is always uncertainty in the employer's mind. Even if a candidate seems absolutely ideal, employers always worry about, 'What if they aren't any good?'

To understand this, you have to see it from the employer's point of view. You may have tested a person's ability to do a job, but 90 per cent of the staff problems organizations have to deal with are not about competence. They're about attitude. Whether staff are competent or not is, to a large extent, up to the organization. Competence problems can be fixed by training, supervision and encouragement. Attitude is up to the individual.

So until a person starts, the employer just doesn't know how they are going to work out. If you can reassure the employer by telling them how enthusiastic you are about the job and how much you want it, you'll be giving them the confidence they need to believe your attitude will be a good one.

Ask For Another Interview

What happens if your interview went reasonably well, but not quite as well as you'd liked? Suppose you meant to ask lots of highly intelligent questions, but when it came to it you dried up? Don't despair. All is not lost. You can always ask for another chance.

Putting yourself through a second interview might be the last thing you feel like doing. To the person who is doing the hiring, having someone call up and say they want to, 'Meet the people in your department', or simply, 'I'd like another chance to come in and talk to you', indicates to them how seriously you want the job. Which can only be a good thing. If your first interview didn't go too well, this tactic may very well put you back in the running.

You might need to come up with a good reason for the organization to invite you back. For instance: 'After our meeting I

Afterwards

realized there were still a few questions I wanted to ask you. I am very interested in the job, and would really like the chance to come in and talk with you again.'

Or how about this: 'When I came in to see you I had rather a bad cold, and because of that I really don't think I did myself justice. I am very interested in the job, and would really like the chance to come in and talk with you again.' I know someone who said just that – he got his second interview and the job.

You don't have to follow up on all these suggestions, but being proactive is infinitely preferable to waiting for the telephone to ring. Success won't just fall into your lap so get up and grab it!

20 Your Second Interview

You've already been to one interview. Now you've been invited back a second time. Second interviews are very common. In fact, it's quite unusual for anyone to be offered a job after just one interview. Since you first met your prospective employer:

- the initial round of interviews has been completed;
- there has been some discussion about the various candidates, including you;
- a short-list has been drawn up.

So Why Do They Want You to Come Back?

Here are some of the reasons.

They Just Want to Have Another Look at You

This is fine. Going along for a second interview gives you the opportunity to take another look at *them*. It gives you a chance to ask the questions you forgot to ask the first time around. It gives you another chance to decide whether you really want to work there.

They've Made a Short-list and Now it's Decision Time

Remember, the interviewer may have already seen a good many people. They'll know which candidates impressed them, and which ones didn't. Choosing between a small number of people is easier than choosing between a large number. That's why they want to see the best people again. Your job is to get them to choose you.

Someone Else in the Organization Wants to See You

If you were interviewed by personnel the first time around, a second interview is likely to be with the department you'll actually be working for. If you've been interviewed by your prospective boss, your second interview might be with them and their boss.

Don't automatically assume that the final decision rests with this new person. The choice might still rest with the person who first interviewed you, they might simply want a second opinion or some reassurance that they are making the right decision.

They Want People in the Office to Meet You

This invitation to meet prospective new colleagues is a very good 'buying signal'. It's a great opportunity for you, too. You want the chance to get to know the people you'll be working with, day in, day out, for the next few years, don't you? Chapters 15 and 18 contain ideas on how to handle this.

They Want Some Reassurance That They've Made the Right Decision

Employers are always extremely worried about making the wrong decision (no matter what their position in the organization is). Inviting you back a second time gives them a further opportunity to reinforce their judgement that you are the right person.

Preparing For the Second Interview

In the same way that you prepared for your first interview, you need to:

- follow the advice previously described in this book on interview technique. You'll need to be even more professional this time, since the people you'll be in competition with are the best of the bunch.

- draw up a detailed checklist of things you want to know about the company and the job itself. You don't want to leave thinking, 'Oh, I wished I'd asked...'

- think about the things you discussed at the first interview. Were there any questions you feel you didn't answer satisfactorily? This may be an area they will return to. Make sure you don't get caught out a second time.

- think of something to say this about? 'When we first met you said such and such. I've been considering this and I think...'

- refresh your memory as to who you saw last time. They'll be flattered if you remember them, and put off if you've completely forgotten they exist.

Your Objective

As far as you are concerned, the purpose of your second interview is to:

- let the organization know that you still really want the job;

- find out what the situation is (more details shortly);

- reinforce their judgement that you are the best person for the job;

- persuade them to offer you the job.

What to Say on the Telephone

If you get a letter inviting you back for a second interview, you'll have to arrange exactly when and where the meeting is to take place. Make sure you have the letter in front of you, and the name of the person who originally interviewed you, before you make the call. When you pick up the telephone:

- Ask to be put through to the person who signed the letter.

- Introduce yourself, and explain why you're calling, 'Hello Mr Brown, it's John West here. I've just received your letter, asking me to come in and see you again.'

- Be enthusiastic. Tell them how pleased you are to be invited back.

- During the course of the conversation, try and get a little more information about the meeting. Who's going to interview you? Will it be the same person as last time, or someone else? If it is someone different, make sure you write the name down so you are prepared.

- Is there anything they want you to bring along?

- If you haven't already had a chance to meet your new colleagues, or look around the department, ask if you can this time.

- Smile as you speak; it shows in your voice and makes you sound friendly.

- At the end of the call, confirm the date and time of the meeting and tell them you're looking forward to seeing them, 'So that's 11 o'clock next Friday morning, 3 May. I look forward to seeing you again.'

What to Wear

What did you wear the first time? It must have been a good choice since they liked you enough to invite you back. In theory, it should be easy to decide what to wear for your second interview. After all, you've already been to the organization's premises and seen what people are wearing.

> **Note:** If the dress code was extremely casual, it's still a good idea to dress smartly for your interview. Leave the jeans and T-shirt until you actually start working there.

In fact, interviewers don't normally take much notice of what you're wearing – unless you look dirty and unkempt, in which case you won't be invited back a second time. As long as you look smart, that's all that counts. And if you only have one 'interview outfit' don't worry about wearing it again. Do you remember what your *interviewer* was wearing?

The Second Interview Begins

So what's the first thing you should say when you walk in the door? Smile and say, 'I was really hoping you'd invite me back. Thank you very much.'

No one could be anything but impressed by that statement. Is has everything going for it. It's respectful, friendly, enthusiastic, and it tells your interviewer that you still really want the job. Everything, in fact, that they were hoping to hear. If you get the same interviewer as the last time, you can say, 'It's great to see you again Mr Brown. I was really hoping you'd invite me back. Thank you very much.' Your Mr Brown will sit down with a great big grin on his face thinking, 'Hey, this guy remembered me. He's all right.' Don't forget to shake their hand either.

What to Say Next

Nothing. After the initial greetings, you really need to keep quiet and listen. This is the point at which the interviewer will do all the talking. This second interview is very much their show. Probably, the first thing that they'll talk about is why you've been invited back. They'll explain that they've finished the initial round of interviews, and that you (lucky you) are on the short-list.

At this stage, there'll be several things you want to know.

- How many other people are there on the short-list?

- How many of them have they already seen/still to see?

- When is the final decision going to be made?

- How are you doing in comparison to the others?

Your interviewer will probably tell you the answers to the first three questions, but not necessarily. If not, you'll just have to ask. The answer to the last question, that of how well you stand in comparison to the others, is unlikely to be volunteered. Be prepared to ask about this.

There are lots of benefits to asking, 'How do I stand in comparison to the other candidates?' For a start, the interviewer will know that you're still interested in the job, that you are anxious to know what your chances are. If you get an answer like, 'Well now it's between you and the candidate we saw last night', you'll know that the job is almost in the bag, but not quite.

> **Note:** It would be a good idea to have a notebook handy, so you can jot down any points which you might want to ask about later.

Reassuring the Employer that You Are the Right Person

As I've said before, employers are always worried about making the wrong decision. At the second interview stage, all the candidates are possible choices, but which one to pick? Unless one particular person stands out, head and shoulders above the rest, it's a very difficult decision. They want someone who:

- really wants the job;
- would be good at the job and or be willing to train;
- fit in with the staff and the organization's culture;
- will stay in the job, not leave after 10 minutes;
- will have a good attitude: work hard, come in on time, take the job seriously, not take loads of time off, and so on.

They can't possibly know all that until the successful candidate starts to work for them. So how can you reassure them that you match all these criteria? The answer is to tell them.

'From everything I've seen, and all we've talked about, I know this job would be a really good move for me.'

'From everything I've seen, and all we've talked about, I know this is the perfect job for me.'

'It all sounds really great. I'd really like to work here.'

'Thanks for giving me the chance to meet the people in the department. They're really friendly. If I'm successful, I know I'll really enjoy working here.'

'This is just what I've been looking for.'

'I know I can do a really good job for you. If you offer me the job, I know you won't be disappointed.'

Do you get the idea? You have to tell them that by picking you, they're making the right decision. When you tell your potential new employer these things, what you're doing is selling to them. You are selling you!

Asking for the Order

This means asking for the job.

'From everything I've seen, and all we've talked about, it sounds perfect. If you want me to, I could start next week.'

Or, 'If you were to offer me the job right now, I'd jump at the chance. What do you think of the idea?'

Or, 'I really want this job'

However you phrase it, the most important thing to do after you've asked for the job, is to shut up. Don't say anything. Even if there is an embarrassingly long silence, or your interviewer falls off their chair in surprise, keep quiet. Whatever you do, make sure it's your interviewer who breaks the silence and not you.

Whatever you do, don't suddenly feel embarrassed and start waffling. Just ask for the job and then be quiet. It's possible you'll be offered the job there and then.

The other possibility is that your interviewer will say that they need some time to think about it. If that's the case, you can always say, 'Is there anything else I can do, or anything else I can tell you, that would influence your decision?'

How to End the Second Interview

Sometimes you can go right through a second interview and still not have any idea how you've fared. Here are one or two things you can ask at the end of the interview, which should give you a few clues. 'When can I expect to hear from you?' If the interviewer says, 'We plan to have a letter to you in the post tonight', or 'I'll give you a ring tomorrow evening', you'll have reason to be hopeful.

If you already know when the last candidate is being seen you could ask whether you can call *them*. Asking, 'Would you mind if I phoned you at 5 pm tomorrow?' is perfectly acceptable. It shows you are keen, and that you're respectful – after all, you are asking their permission. It also puts the ball very firmly in your court. Just make sure you do call exactly when you said you would.

Word of Warning

Whatever happens during your second interview, remember the job is not in the bag yet. You are still being judged every moment you're there. The decision to hire is very unlikely to be made until after you've left, and probably not until all the other short-listed candidates have been seen. So be confident, but don't be conceited.

21 Creating a Second Chance

Your application has been unsuccessful. Now what? Nobody has a 100 per cent success record when it comes to job-hunting. (If you meet someone who tells you otherwise – they're lying.) However, if you've tried and failed a number of times, it's time to turn detective. At what stage in the recruitment process were you turned down?

Failing at the Paper Stage

If you never get any further than sending in your CV or application form, perhaps it's time for a rethink about the way you presented yourself on paper.

- Re-read the chapters in this book on CVs, covering letters and application forms to try and find out where you're going wrong.

- Show the CV and copies of application forms you've sent out to your friends and your careers service. Ask for their honest opinion. Can they spot mistakes you've missed?

- What about the presentation of the material? Does it look good, or is there room for improvement?

- Did you apply well before the closing dates? Did you send your application to the right place? Are you putting the correct postage on your envelope?

- Think about the jobs for which you've been applying. From the information you give, do you look like a suitable candidate? Do you have the right qualifications or experience, interest or personality? Be honest. Are you applying for jobs you couldn't possibly land?

- Is there simply too much competition? Many large organizations receive hundreds of applications for every vacancy they advertise. Increase your chances of success by applying to smaller companies, on spec as well as in response to advertised positions.

Failing at the Interview Stage

What happens if you always seem to fly through the initial stages of the recruitment process, but always get a polite letter of rejection after the interview? If this is happening, you'll know the 'you' you present on paper is acceptable. It's your interview technique that's letting you down. Or is it? The best way to find out is to ask for feedback. You might be surprised.

Finding Out What Went Wrong

This might be the last thing you feel like doing, but wouldn't it be a good idea to find out where you've been going wrong? Even if the feedback sounds negative it's still immensely invaluable to you. What you have to do is screw up the courage, telephone or write to the person who interviewed you and ask, 'Why didn't I get the job?'

Making the Telephone Call

Introduce yourself, and remind the interviewer of the date you met and the job they interviewed you for. Tell them how disappointed you were not to be successful, and ask whether they wouldn't mind giving you some feedback on why your application was rejected. Was it your interview technique? Was there something that you said (or did) that put them off?

> **Tip:** Make sure you are always polite, friendly and appreciative when you ask for feedback. If you are aggressive, you won't get anywhere.

Getting honest feedback also depends upon the personality of the person you're speaking to. They might be quite happy to tell you that you didn't get the job because you looked like you hadn't had a bath in three years. Then again, if that really was the reason they might be too embarrassed to say.

If you get the feeling they don't want to upset you, make it clear that you really don't mind them being unflattering or negative, you just want to know so you can improve next time. It's never too late to learn from your mistakes.

What if You Didn't Do Anything Wrong?

What happens when you're told, 'We had so many good candidates it was a very difficult decision to make. I'm sorry you were unsuccessful', or 'In the end, we had to decide between you and one other person. I'm sorry, but we ended up choosing them.'

This is a much more positive discovery. If you hadn't asked for feedback, you might still be nursing a bruised ego, but now your rejection can be looked at in a different light. Now you have a chance to 'keep your foot in the door', or even land a job – yes, it is possible even at this stage.

Keeping Your Foot in the Door

If it appears that you've only just missed landing the job, why not ask whether there are other vacancies coming up in the near future. Say that when you came in for interview, you were impressed by what you saw and you'd still really like to work for them. Since employers need reassurance that they've picked the right person for the job, and since they're always on the lookout for people who really want to work for them, this will be music to their ears.

Lots of vacancies are filled this way. Just think; they've already interviewed you and they liked what they saw. Next time they need someone, you could be just the person.

Speak to Their Personnel Department

If the organization has a personnel or human resources department, speak to them too. Even though you've failed to secure this particular job, you *did* make it to the final stages of the selection process. Tell them how much you want to work for their organization (especially since you've had a chance to come in and see it for yourself) and ask for information on other vacancies.

Are there any other vacancies available now? Do they know what's coming up in the near future? Perhaps there's a similar job to the one you applied for in a different department?

Personnel staff are usually friendly and helpful. If you telephone them regularly, you might be in just the right place at the right time, next time.

Keeping in Touch

If there isn't anything available immediately, ask the company to keep your CV or application form on file, and to call you if anything does come up.

Even better, be proactive and ask whether you can call them back in a month's time. If they agree, make sure you do. It really does pay to be persistent. In that time, another vacancy might have opened up. Or the person who beat you to the job might not be working out. They should have hired you in the first place and now is their big chance!

Being Cheeky

This example is from my own personal experience, and proves victory can be snatched from the jaws of defeat. On being turned down for a job, I called the company to find out why. I was told the decision had been between me and just one other person. Apparently we'd both been so good, the decision had been made by flipping a coin!

'Why not hire us both?' I said, in a moment of madness. And they did!

If I can do it, you can too. Never give up.

22 Landing the Job

The telephone rings, you can't believe your ears. 'We'd like to offer you the job.' Great! And that really is the end of the book. Except there are one or two more things to say, such as how to reply to a job offer, and how to negotiate your 'package'.

Replying to a Job Offer

If you are offered a job over the telephone, ask the organization to confirm their offer in writing. Once you have the letter it is customary to reply, thanking them and accepting the position. When you write your letter, remember to mention how much you are looking forward to working with them. Give them a nice warm feeling before you even start.

What if I'm Still Waiting to Hear From Another Organization?

It is bad form to accept a job and then change your mind. Be sure you really do want the job before you post that letter of acceptance.

If you've been offered one job, but the organization you *really* want to work for hasn't contacted you, this is what to do. Telehone the one you haven't heard from yet, and ask them for their help. Tell them you've received another offer (don't tell them who from) and that you are reluctant to accept it until you know what *they* are going to decide. Make it crystal clear you'd much rather work for them; that their job is the one you really want. Ask them what your chances are, and when can you expect to hear from them.

If you play your cards right, you could come away from the conversation holding a second offer, and at the very least, an indication of when you can expect the decision.

Start Dates

When do you want to start working? Next Monday, next month, next year? Once an organization has made the decision to employ somebody, they usually want them to start as soon as possible.

Start dates are usually discussed during the interview, so by the time you've received an offer you'll have a pretty good idea of when the organization wants you to start, and they'll have a pretty good idea of what you want too. If a start date is not mentioned in your offer, phone up and discuss it.

What if There is No Choice?

Many large organizations, especially those taking on large numbers of new recruits, start everyone on the same day. You'll be given the start date, the start time, and that will be that. The reason is simple. It's cheaper to train a group of people than one individual.

On the plus side, they'll probably have a very professional programme lined up which you wouldn't want to miss by starting three weeks later.

Salary

You probably discussed salary at your interview, but what if the amount you've been offered isn't as much as you were hoping for? Chapter 1 covered the ways to research salaries in your chosen profession. Have you done this? Are your expectations realistic?

If you're really unhappy, ring up and discuss it. Tell them how you feel, tell them what you were expecting. Although you are in a strong position (assuming you haven't accepted the job yet) avoid asking for a figure miles above the going rate or you'll just be disappointed.

Of course, as with start dates, there may not be any room for manoeuvre. Those same organizations that start everyone off on the same day, usually pay new recruits the same as each other as well.

Some organizations operate a grading system; your salary is determined by your grade. I know of one organization that pays absolutely everyone the same salary, from the most senior manager right down to the most junior member of staff. You can see it pays to have done your research.

The 'Perks'

Never turn down a job on the basis of salary until you've considered the entire package. These are some of the things you could be offered:

- excellent holiday entitlement;

- flexible working hours;

- flexible working arrangements eg, working from home;

- generous sickness pay;

- generous maternity pay and childcare facilities (useful if you're planning a family);

- annual and performance related bonuses;

- profit sharing;

- company car;

- mobile phone;

- pension entitlements;

- sports and social clubs;

- company trips to exotic places – yes some companies do offer this!

- travel concessions;

- season ticket;

- cheaper mortgages and other loans;

- subsidized or free meals;

- discounts on the organization's products.

There may be many more, depending on the industry you'll be working in, and the job itself. It may also be easier to negotiate additional perks than basic salary.

Conclusion

During your job hunt, you've been on your best behaviour. You've been polite and courteous, you've been friendly, and you've worked really hard. Above all, you've acted in the most professional manner that you know how. It's just as well because now the practice is going to come in handy!

From now on you'll be working on becoming indispensable – but that's another story. Congratulations on landing a job, be happy, and remember to turn up on time!

Further Reading From Kogan Page

Get the Job You Want in 30 Days, Gary Joseph Grappo, 1998

Great Answers to Tough Interview Questions, Martin John Yate, 4th edition, 1998

How to Master Personality Questionnaires, Mark Parkinson, 1997

How to Master Psychometric Tests, Mark Parkinson, 1997

How to Pass Selection Tests, Mike Bryant and Sanjay Modha, 2nd edition, 1998

How You Can Get That Job! Application forms and letters made easy, Rebecca Corfield, 2nd edition, 1999

Interviews Made Easy, Mark Parkinson, 2nd edition, 1999

Marketing Yourself and Your Career, Jane Ballback and Jan Slater, 1998

Net that Job! Using the World Wide Web to develop your career and find work, Irene Krechowiecka, 1998

Preparing Your Own CV, Rebecca Corfield, 2nd edition, 1999

Readymade CVs, Lynn Williams, 1996

Readymade Interview Questions, Malcolm Peel, 2nd edition, 1996

Further Reading From Kogan Page

Readymade Job Search Letters, Lynn Williams, 1995

Successful Interview Skills, Rebecca Corfield, 2nd edition, 1999

30 Minutes Before Your Job Interview, June Lines, 1997

30 Minutes to Prepare a Job Application, June Lines, 1997

Index

application forms 38–43
asking for the order 163–64, 178
asking questions 156–59
audio–visual aids 113–15
    flip charts 114–15
    overhead projectors 112–13

body language
    face to face 129–31
    on the telephone 48
    smiling 48, 160

careers 1–7, 15, 20
careers offices 5, 7, 12, 15
Chamber of Commerce 5
charity work 30, 32, 139
chickening out 123
commitment questions 138–39
competency questions 39, 139–41
computer literacy 29
covering letters 50–57
    content 53–55
    on spec 85–87
    presentation 50–53
CVs 24–27, 58–75
CV writing services 74–75

discrimination 67, 143–46

dress, how to 120–21, 174
drinking 132–33

eating 48, 133
e–mail 24–29, 86
expenses, claiming 133
eye contact 130, 160

failing
    at interview 180
    at paper stage 179–80
feedback, asking for 164, 166–68, 180–81
friends\family 4, 6, 16–17

gap year 30–31
graduate
    employers 13
    newspapers 10
    recruitment agencies 20–21
group exercises 104–08

handshakes 130–31
holiday work 31, 139
honesty 41, 73, 102, 134, 138

In tray exercises 103–05
Internet 5, 7, 18–29
    access 28

Index

chat rooms 22
e–mail 24–29
employer sites 21–22
interesting sites 5, 9, 19–21, 25
on–line applications 23–24
virtual CVs 24–27
interviews 44–49, 117–64, 170–78
  questions 134–46
interviewers, different types 147–52
introductions 126–29, 131–32

job offers 184–87
job satisfaction 5

key words 23–24

local papers 8–9

Milk Round 12–13
money 3
multiple choice questions 39–41

national papers 5, 9–10
networking 16–17

one–to–one interviews 117
'on spec' applications 76–88
other people 125–26, 160–61

panel interviews 117–118
part–time work 30–32
'perks' 186–87
photographs 25, 67
placements, *see* work placements

popular questions 135–38
presentations 108–14
problem–solving exercises 107–08
Prospects Today 10–11, 20
psychometric tests 94–102
  numerical reasoning 97–100
  personality 100–102
  verbal reasoning 94–97
punctuality 123–25

recruitment agencies 4, 15–16, 18–21
recruitment fairs 11–12
  Milk Round 12
  SME fairs 15
references 72–73
researching
  careers 6–7
  companies 33–35
  for interviews 120
  job content 36
  salaries 4–5
  why do it? 33–34

Sainsbury's 13, 40
salary 4, 185–87
second interviews 168–69, 170–78
small to medium sized enterprises (SMEs) 13–15
smoking 48, 133
specialist magazines 10
speculative applications, *see* 'on spec'
swearing 132

Index

taking notes 159–60
telephone interviews 44–49
tracking your application 92, 167
trade magazines 10
trick questions 141–42
two-to-one interviews 117

vacation work, *see* holiday work

video-conferencing 115–16
virtual CVs 24–27
voluntary work 32, 139

work experience 114–15
work placements 30–31
work shadowing 7